Dachshunds

DACHSHUNDS

AN OWNER'S COMPANION

Elizabeth Heesom

HOWELL
BOOK HOUSE
New York

MAXWELL MACMILLAN CANADA
Toronto

MAXWELL MACMILLAN INTERNATIONAL
New York Oxford Singapore Sydney

Howell Book House
Macmillan Publishing Company
866 Third Avenue
New York, NY 10022

Maxwell Macmillan Canada, Inc.
1200 Eglinton Avenue East, Suite 200
Don Mills, Ontario M3C 3N1

Macmillan Publishing Company is part of the Maxwell Communication Group of Companies.

Library of Congress Cataloging-in-Publication Data

Heesom, Elizabeth.
    Dachshunds: an owner's companion/Elizabeth Heesom.
    p.m.
    Originally published: Ramsbury, Wiltshire, England: Crowood Press, 1991
    Includes index.
    ISBN 0–87605–133–6
    1. Dachshund.   I. Title.
SF429.D25H44 1992   91–27511
636.7'53--dc20   CIP

Acknowledgements
The author would like to thank the following people for kindly supplying photographs for this book. Gibbs for the photographs on pages 46, 70 and 180 (top); Mitchell for those on pages 50 and 182 (bottom); Fountain for those on pages 52, 56, 60, 64, 100, 178 (top) and 187 (top); Fall for those on pages 71, 123 and 180 (bottom); Turner for those on pages 82, 85, 90, 105, 182 (top) and 189; Maher for those on pages 87, 131 and 179; Bamber for page 89; Garwood for page 133; Cooke for page 176; Walker for page 181; and Hartley for page 187 (bottom).

Macmillan books are available at special discounts for bulk purchases for sales promotions, premiums, fund-raising, or educational use. For details, contact:

Special Sales Director
Macmillan Publishing Company
866 Third Avenue
New York, NY 10022

10 9 8 7 6 5 4 3 2 1

Printed in Great Britain

Contents

	Acknowledgements	6
1	The History of the Dachshund	7
2	The Standard	45
3	The Pedigree	76
4	Selecting Your Dachshund	81
5	Puppy Management	88
6	Adolescent and Adult Care	97
7	Training Your Dachshund	106
8	Making a Start in the Show-ring	122
9	Breeding	130
10	Pre-Natal Care and Whelping	141
11	Ailments and Diseases	159
12	Famous Dogs Around the World	167
13	Conclusion	174
	Appendix Important Pedigrees	191
	Useful Addresses	220
	Index	223

Acknowledgements

I am very grateful to all those who have given me information and encouragement whilst compiling this book; to Pam Sydney (Yatesbury) for reading through my script, to Betty Beaumont (Longanlow) for lending me so much of her valued material, to Irmgard Schulze and Inge Seidenbusch for their research into Dachshunds in Germany today, to Mr J.B.A. Davies BSc BVM & MRCVS for his helpful notes, to Val Beynon (Brockbane) for her article on Dachshunds in obedience, to John Gallop (Rhinefields), for his article on the pedigree, and to all those numerous people who have let me have photographs, especially Margaret Turner (Marictur), Mr Maher (Landelf), Mr Fountain and so many more.

1

The History of the Dachshund

Early History

It is undoubtedly to the German forester, in his dark green uniform and feather in cap, that we owe our beloved Dachshund, or 'Teckel'. The word Teckel (or Dachel or Dachsel), is used extensively throughout Germany and her neighbouring countries, and is derived from the original form of Dachshund (Badger dog), through a process of word change – Dachsel, Dachel, Teckel and so forth are diminutives, in the same way as Hans and Grete became Hansel and Gretel. The suggestion that Teckel arose from the State of Teck in Germany seems unlikely, as the word Teck has been widely used in the origin of the Dachshund. The foresters all over that vast country, and particularly in the east, where there were such huge forests, were busy perfecting him for the tough work which they demanded of him.

Long before the aristocracy of Europe fell in love with this bright little hunter, the foresters had developed him, and moulded him to their heart's desire – a brave, robust and intelligent worker. He could go to ground or trail above ground through thick undergrowth, and, obstinate to the last, hold his prey at bay, barking in order to bring his master to the scene in order to finish off the prey, which would sometimes be fox or badger, sometimes rabbit or fierce wild boar, all of which abounded in the seventeenth and eighteenth centuries.

The Dachshund-type dog, long in back and low to ground with a hound-like head, goes back centuries earlier than that, and a similar dog is described and sometimes depicted in most accounts of the hunt, as early as the fourteenth century, or before.

Claims that the Dachshund originated in ancient Egypt, made on the basis of an inscription found on a tablet in Thebes, depicting a king with a small dog at his feet, and the word *Tekel*, are obviously romantic, yet there *were* undoubtedly dogs of a Dachshund type in

7

*Some of the old stamp of Dachshund were much more of the Terrier
type than those of today, and many resembled the Bassett Hound.*

ancient Egypt, and dogs of this type were also described in ancient Greece, as well as all over Europe. Those poor turnspit dogs, described by Thomas Bewick, the great naturalist in 1792, fit the bill, they sound very Dachshund-like, and some were even dappled.

Many of the early hunting books give delightful names to those pioneers; *Lockhundlein* (little burrow dog), *Erdhundle* (little earth dog), *Schlifferlin* (little burrower), *Dachsschlieffer* (badger burrower) etc., and without doubt these little dogs were the ancestors of our Dachshunds.

In 1719 the German authority Fleming gave us a graphic account of a dog he called the *Dachskriecker* – a special kind of earth dog, used as a burrower, small and long and slender in body, with short feet, slightly bent and useful for digging. He said that these dwarfs, although so small, were exceedingly zealous and brave, and would work to the limit of their capacity. They would burrow, drive and track their prey, give tongue and hold them at bay. Fleming also describes these dogs as being usually red or blackish, with pendant ears like a hound.

Such small dogs are often described in the early hunting books in France. The writer Buffon, in his *Histoire Naturelle* in 1793, described a dog very like those early Dachshunds; and there is the famous woodcut from *La Vénerie de Jacques du Fouilloux*, dated 1561, showing small, low-legged, drop-eared dogs going to earth, encouraged by a rakish looking youth in doublet and hose. Although these hounds do not greatly resemble our modern Dachshunds, nevertheless a resemblance *is* there.

The French *bas-set* (from whence Basset comes), really just means low-set, and their name for the Dachshund was 'Bassets de Race Allemande'. In Denmark the Dachshund is the 'Gravhund' (earth dog), and in Poland the 'Jamnik' (hole dog), showing how the fact of going to ground was of paramount importance in defining the dog.

One could continue to give accounts from all over Europe of short-legged hound-like dogs of various colours and coats being used for the hunt, but the real story begins around the middle half of the eighteenth century, when Dachshunds were bred seriously and developed by the foresters in Germany in order to contain the vast numbers of foxes, badgers, rabbits, etc., in the huge forests of that country, and to give sport to the many landowners. One of the Teckel's first ancestors seems to have been the *Bracke*, also called the *Dachsbracke*. Although this dog is very much heavier, and longer-legged than the Teckel, doubtless shorter-legged and smaller

Early German Dachshunds.

specimens were selected for breeding. Various other crosses were introduced to improve the performance, and undoubtedly one of the most important and lasting in its effect was the introduction, by von Daake (who lived in the region of the Harz mountains), of bloodhound strains. This cross was indeed a great triumph for our breed, accounting for the wonderful scenting ability of the Dachshund, and which renders him truly unique among the smaller hunters. This ability has often astonished the uninformed at scenting tests. The bloodhounds which von Daake used, around 1820, were a smaller, shorter-legged type than the present English bloodhounds, and were called Harzen Bloodhounds, or sometimes *Schweisshunde*.

Much has been written about the origins of the Wire and the Long-haired Dachshunds. It seems fairly certain that the wire coat was a product of crossings with German Pinchers, and with some strains of Dandie Dinmont terriers, the latter cross being blamed for soft coats, so often a problem in Wire Dachshunds, as the standard calls for a short harsh, tough *wire* coat.

The long-haired variety has been credited with the introduction of Spaniel blood, although there is much evidence to suggest the introduction of *Wachtelhund* blood, a native German dog, used mostly for quail hunting. The long-haired and the wire-haired varieties were considered to be more useful for overland work,

10

Miss Wendy Riley's pack of Dachshunds at work.

trailing game and *surlaut* or giving tongue, than the smooth-haired, who was predominantly an earth dog. The long coat has the disadvantage of collecting earth when working underground, but he has the advantage over his smooth brother when working in water.

In the past, and indeed right up to the present day, the wire-haired Dachshund excelled in hunting overland. His low stature and strong dense coat rendered him ideal for thrusting through thick undergrowth in the forests, and for trailing and *totverbeling* (giving tongue), over dead game. Today he is still used to hunt wild boar in the forests of Germany. A small dog, but with the heart and courage of a lion!

The foresters discarded any dogs found unsuitable for work, and many of these Dackels went as pets, often to the household of the master for whom the forester worked. This was the beginning of a great rise in popularity of the Dachshund as a household companion as well as a hunter. This versatile little hound possessed a genius for adapting itself to a life of luxury within the grandeur of the

11

Treue Freunde, by Theodor Kleehaas. Now in Leipzig.

Schloss. For better or worse, the Dachshund had come to stay. Centuries later and after two wars with his homeland, the Dachshund, when all the six varieties of coats and sizes are added together, heads the list of registrations in the Hound Group in Great Britain.

It was during the First World War, that the following delightful verses by Patrick Chalmers appeared in *Punch*:

'No good thing comes out of Kaiserland,'
Says Phyllis; but beside the fire I note
One Wilhelm, sleek in tawny gold of coat,
Most satin-smooth to the caresser's hand.

A velvet mien; an eye of amber, full
of that which keeps the faith with us for life;
Lover of meal-times; Hater of yard-dog strife;
Lordly with silken ears most strokeable.

Familiar on the hearth, refuting her,
He sits, the antic-pawed, the proven friend,
The whimsical, the grave and reverend –
Wilhelm the Dachs from out of Hanover.

12

In the early nineteenth century in Germany whilst the foresters were still breeding and using their dogs for work, the Dachshund was gaining all the time in popularity as a pet, and he began to appear at shows.

The German Standard

In 1879 a list of desirable characteristics was drawn up, which later became the basis of the present day standard. In that year fifty-four Dachshund entries appeared in the first German Stud Book, including many of the great names in Dachshund history. One of these was Wilhelm von Daake, son of August von Daake, who had such an influence on the breed. Wilhelm was amongst those first owners to be listed. His main object was to breed a dog capable of working both above and below ground, and the ideal weights that he aimed for were between 17–18lb (7.5–8kg) for a male, and 14–15lb (6–7kg) for a female. This is interesting, as today, in Great Britain, the weight of nearly all Standard Dachshunds would be well over 20lb (9kg), and some would be almost 30lb (13.5kg).

Today in Germany instead of our two sizes (Miniatures of 11lb (5kg) or under, and Standards of 20–26lb (9–12kg)), there are *three* weight classes – heavy, average and miniature. The heavy males are more than 15lb (7kg) and females 14lb (6.5kg). Average males are under 15lb (7kg) and females under 14lb (6.5kg). Miniature males are under 9lb (4kg) and females under 7.5lb (3.5kg). Quaint little Teckels these are but, I understand, full of courage and true Dachshund character.

In the very first standard drawn up by the German Teckelklub, the word 'gnomenhaft', gnome-like, was used to describe the Dachshund, although later on this word was dropped from the standard. Nevertheless an aura of fairy-tale quality lingered around the Dachshund; he was a puckish figure, dwelling in the forests, and an ideal subject for cartoons and affectionate ridicule, not only in Germany, but in his many adopted countries.

The German Teckelklub was founded in 1888 by Major Ilgner and Lieutenant Count Hahn. The club arranged special breed shows, arranged burrow tests, and held regular meetings to discuss aspects and problems of the breed. Soon after this, several regional clubs in places like Frankfurt, Munich, and other large cities were also started, so great was the rise in popularity of the Teckel. He had in fact crept out of his forest haunts, and had rapidly adapted himself to a life of luxury in cities and the home.

That the Dachshund might lose his hunting instincts and ability began to worry a great many enthusiasts, and in 1905 a group of hunters met in a small town near Wittenburg and formed *Der Deutsche Jagdteckelklub*, which was soon followed by *Der Gebrauchsteckelklub* in 1909. This body soon had affiliated clubs all over Germany, their object being to preserve the hunting instincts of the breed, and they established their own special stud book, for working dogs who had passed their tests.

The dogs who had been successfully examined at hunting trials and tests were (and are still today), given *Leistungszeichen*, which are added ever afterwards to their name. Examples include:

Bh F K	Dog has been examined at fox earth.
BI B K	Dog has been examined at badger kennel (artificial).
BH D N	Dog has been examined at badger sett (natural).
SP	'Spurlaut' means the dog barks on trail.
Schwh. K	Dog has been examined and follows blood on artificial trail.
TW	Dog leads to the dead game.
W	'Wurgler' means strangler; the dog would seize his prey by the throat and hold it until the hunter arrived.

These are just a few of the letters which a good hunter might have added to his name. A registered dog's name might read thus: Weitstein Klaus 6875303 R Bh D N.

The 'Wurgler', or strangler, would not necessarily finish off the prey himself. One of his main functions was to flush the prey from the burrow, so that the hunter could deal with it, or the other dogs waiting above ground would take over. My own experience is that Dachshunds work well in this respect without any special training and, it seems to be inbred in them. In Africa, I had a great many Dachshunds roaming loose on our farm, and they became great hunters. I found that the self-appointed pack leader, (a Von der Howitt import from England), would start work on a burrow, digging and then pulling out roots with his teeth, then he would stand back and let his underlings take over and continue until they had flushed out the prey – usually the large, fierce mole rat, who possesses Dracula-like fangs – he would then step in, take over, and render the *coup de grâce*.

One of the most important of the early German breeders was without doubt Dr Fritz Engelmann. His Von Sonnenstein dogs, smooth, wire and long-haired, have had a permanent influence on the Teckel. Dr Engelmann preferred the active, lighter type of dog above all others, and devoted a great deal of time and energy to breeding a distemper-free animal, mostly by mating dogs which had suffered from this terrible disease, and had recovered from it. How thankful we should be today for the scientific progress made in animal husbandry that has allowed us to have our dogs inoculated against this awful disease. In Engelmann's day years of loving work and effort could be literally wiped out in one fell swoop.

Some of the dogs which Dr Engelmann greatly admired were from the Gib-Hals kennel, bred by Paul Selchow, who worked towards the development of a lightweight hunter. Today his dogs would not be given a second glance in a show-ring, unless it were one of horror and amazement. They were, according to contemporary account, short in body, high on the leg, light in bone and short in head. Despite the general dislike of the small and nimble 'Gibhalser' type of Dachshund, Selchow's sincere aims were understood and respected by his colleagues, and after his death in 1928, annual field trials bearing his name were established as a memorial to him.

Fortunately Dr Engelmann has left us a wealth of literature on the Dachshund, and it is to him that we are indebted for so much of our knowledge of the breed. I think that to understand and to love the Dachshund in all his aspects it is important to know about his early history, and sometimes to forgive him for those characteristics which we try to change. His courage, persistance and very great intelligence were all bred into him for the hunt – he is indeed a small dog with the heart of a lion.

Jester, writing in 1797 said that: 'The Dachshund is of all the hunting dogs the smallest and weakest, but he surpasses them all in courage.' The early standard of the Dachshund in this country stated that he should be 'bold to the point of foolhardiness', and I think that it is a fair description of his character, even today.

Dachshunds in Britain

The Dachshund Club in Great Britain was founded in 1881. It preceded the formation of the German Teckelklub by eight years, proof of how immensely popular this little dog had become.

Four enthusiasts met on 17 July 1881, at Cox's Hotel in Jermyn Street, London, in order to found the club. The four were Major Harry Jones, the Reverend G.F. Lovell, Mr William Arkwright and Mr Montague Wooten, all of whom had successfully bred and owned Dachshunds.

The rise in popularity was due in no small measure to the fact that they were 'Royal Dogs'; Prince Albert had brought two with him to England in 1840, and Queen Victoria owned one in 1845, named 'Deckel'. The Prince Consort in fact imported several, some of which came from the kennels of Prince Edward of Saxe-Weimer, and they were used successfully for pheasant shoots in Windsor Forest.

Queen Victoria was to own Dachshunds all her life, and little tombstones and statues were erected to their memory on their death. There is a wonderful early photograph of Her Majesty and her dear old 'Dacko' lying at her feet on the regal crinoline skirt. He appears to be a small, rather portly red.

A great many of the early imports would very likely have been gifts to guests returning from hunting parties in Germany, and quite possibly a few British dogs remained behind in that country, there

One of Mr Schuller's numerous imports into England from Germany during the 1840s, called Fritz, and sold to Mr F. Barclay, who was one of the earliest Dachshund enthusiasts in England.

being no restriction in those days on the movement of dogs from country to country. Certainly many of the early Dachshund owners were noble; names recorded from this period include the Earl of Onslow, Lord Craven, Lord Ker, Lady Gage and Lady Folkstone, as well as the Prince of Wales, and of course, Her Majesty. They were popular, too, with the artistic set, one of the most famous early owners being the poet (and Head of Rugby School), Matthew Arnold, who was to write a great number of poems to his many Dachsie friends; one of these, *Kaiser Dead*, written in April 1887, has often been quoted, particularly this one little verse:

> Six years ago I brought him down,
> A baby dog, from London town;
> Round his small throat of black and brown
>   A ribbon blue,
> And vouch'd by glorious renown
>   A dachshund true.

But there is, alas, more to this poem, and I quote it here:

> His mother, most majestic dame,
> Of blood-unmixed, from Potsdam came;
> And Kaiser's race we deemed the same –
>   No lineage higher,
> And so he bore the imperial name.
>   But ah, his sire!
>
> Soon, soon the days conviction bring.
> The collie hair, the collie swing,
> The tail's indomitable ring,
>   The eye's unrest –
> The case was clear; a mongrel thing
>   Kai stood confest.

Despite this disgrace dear Kai lived beloved in the Arnold household with the other Dachshunds, and was honoured thus in verse at his death, as was his companion, Geist, whose lineage apparently was without stain.

It is possible that Matthew Arnold acquired his dogs from a Mr Schuller, who lived in Poland Street, London and who seems to have carried on a thriving business importing and selling Dachshunds. It was he, in fact, who imported the black-and-tan dog, Dessaur, who was to become the first British Champion. Dessaur was bred in Germany by Count Pickler, he was out of Waldine by Waldmann, and was owned by Mrs P. Merrik Hoare, of Devon.

It seems that the very first Dachshunds to be exhibited in this country were Carl and Grete, exhibited at a show in Birmingham in 1866, in a class called 'An Extra Class for any Known Breed of Sporting Dog'. Carl and Grete were bred in Germany by Count Knyphauser, and were imported and owned by Mr H. Corbet of Shropshire, one of the famous early pioneers.

Before 1874 Dachshunds were shown in 'Classes for Foreign Dogs', and were usually described as 'German Badger Hounds'. In 1874 the Kennel Club, in the first issue of their Stud Book, recognized the breed, and described them as Dachshunds (or German Badger Hounds).

It has been suggested that the English mis-translation of the German word *hund*, meaning dog, into the word hound, has resulted in the wide difference in type between Dachshunds on the continent and those in Britain today. The British evolved a larger, more hound-like type than the smaller lighter, continental type. This is an argument that has been going on since the very early days, and the first books never seemed to decide the issue, although the pioneer breeders in Britain disagreed happily together. Everett Millais felt very strongly on the subject of the terrier type, and he wrote: 'That there were dogs, and alas, too many of them, with fine bone, Terrier sterns, Terrier heads, and light crooked legs, I will not deny; but, at the same time, I say that they are mongrels. They have got a root in this country, and it will always be my endeavour to eradicate it on every opportunity. The Dachshund proper is a hound, and a little beauty, too. It is very easy to breed a Terrier from a hound, but it is impossible to breed a hound from a Terrier.' The Rev G.F. Lovell, on the other hand, stated (about 1889): 'They may be divided into three varieties – the Hound, the Terrier, and the Toy, although of course these are crossed with one another. The first of these is more generally recognized in the south of England, the second in the north. The third breed which seems chiefly to come from Hanover and the adjacent countries, is distinguished by its snipey jaw, broad flat head, and small size.'

In Cassell's *Book of the Dog*, 1890 we find the following rather nice description from the pen of Mr Enoch Hutton, owner of the immortal Festus. He writes: 'One of the early pioneers of Dachshund lore in England was Mr John Fisher, who had much experience as a breeder and as a judge. Mr Fisher's unrivalled old dog, Feldmann, was also the pioneer of his race on the show-bench in this country, in the days when even the judges had to be educated and enlightened as to the breed and utility of such an animal. I have myself heard a judge of some repute in the canine show-ring give it as his opinion that old Feldmann was nothing but a bad-bred bandy-legged Beagle!'

There is no doubt that today the British-type Dachshund and the continental-type Dachshund *do* vary, although we have only to look at past history to know that they all have sprung from the same roots. I suggest that it must therefore be a matter of selection, originating from the judges in the ring. Both types do exist here, and I am certain that both types exist in Germany as well, but fashion has made us select one type. Those smaller, lighter, perhaps even slightly roached-back pups that occur in our litters we sell as pets, and hope never to see them in the show-ring!

The Original Club

To return briefly to the original Gang of Four who started the Dachshund Club. Mr Arkwright was interested in most sporting dogs, and he bred a great many winners. Major Harry Jones had

Champion Rebecca Celeste of Albaney by Champion Imber Café au Lait out of Anita Celeste of Albaney.

many dogs, too, and the most famous is without doubt the great Champion Jackdaw, who was born in July 1886 out of Wagtail, by Charkov. This dog has become a legend and today one of our most cherished trophies (that awarded to the top winning Smooth of the year, donated by the Dachshund Club) bears his name.

Major Jones was elected the first President of the Club. The Rev Lovell owned several imported dogs, and he was one of the very earliest exhibitors, and Mr Wooten was to become the first Secretary of the Club. He also owned and imported many Dachshunds, many of whom appear to have been reds, and several were described as 'blood red'.

About 1889 the first prefixes started to appear in the Stud Book. Mr Arkwright's prefix was Scarsdale, and some early ones were Alderley, Duckmanton, Kilmanock, and so on.

The 'First Exhibition of Dachshunds and Basset Hounds' was held at the Royal Aquarium Hall, Westminster, in 1886. It was a three-day show, and there were two judges, Mr Montague Wooten judging Dachshunds, and Mr Everett Millais judging Basset Hounds. The total entry was thirty-six – one is left to wonder on how they filled in the time!

Dapples were imported from Germany fairly early on, where they have always been more popular than they are in Britain, and special classes were provided for them. At Alexandra Palace in 1900 there were classes for 'White, Dappled, Brindle and Piebald'. A few Wire-haired were also imported in those early days as well as Smooths, and at Guildford in 1894, as well as the usual Dapple class, there was a class for 'Rough-coated', which was won by Woolsack. He and his descendants Whiskers, Wadding, Wilful, Billy Barlow and Taurus were also winners, and their records are to be found in the early Stud Books. This variety seems to have been largely encouraged by Captain and Mrs Barry, and rough, flat and long-coated classes were scheduled until the First World War. In Cassell's *Book of the Dog*, published in 1890, there is a picture of four dogs which is captioned 'Rough-coated Dachshunds.' In this same book appears the comment: 'The quaint shape and peculiar appearance of the Dachshund rendered him from the first conspicuous on the bench, and greatly influenced many breeders to take up the breed.'

One of those early breeders, the Rev G.F. Lovell of St. Edmund Hall, Oxford, became a great authority on the breed. His first two Dachshunds registered at the Kennel Club were Satan (previously owned by a Mr Forbes, and imported from Stuttgart) and a prize

A typical pre-war champion.

winner in 1869, and Mouse, born in 1872. Both are described as red and 'white'.

There is a famous illustration in Cassell's *Book of the Dog*, showing three smooth-haired Dachshunds, two red and one black-and-tan, and the caption states that they are Festus, the property of Mr Enoch Hutton; Waldmann, the property of Major Cooper; and Schlupferle, the property of the Rev G.F. Lovell. From the picture you can see that Schlupferle, a bright red, has a large white patch on her chest. All three dogs have very crooked front feet, roached backs, and their tails appear quite bushy. What however strikes me from this picture, and from so many other early prints of Dachshunds, are their excellent heads. They would certainly not be amiss in the ring today.

At the Crystal Palace in 1873 (a four-day show), there were the first separate classes for Dachshunds. The winners were: 1st, Mr Hodge's Erdmann; 2nd, Rev Lovell's Satan; and 3rd, Hon. G. Lascelles' Schnaps. All three dogs were imported from Germany. By 1874, there were many shows at which colours were separated. There were classes for Dachshunds Red, Dachshunds other than Red, Dachshunds Black-and-Tan, and Dachshunds other than Black-and-Tan.

Festus, the red dog owned by Mr Enoch Hutton, who came from Pudsey, Leeds, and whose picture appeared in Cassell's book, was one of the first big winners. He was born in 1872, by Mr Fisher's Feldmann out of Waldein, and he was shown only in 1875 and 1876, but during this time he won forty-seven prizes and two cups.

At the Alexandra Palace in 1877 there were separate classes for dogs under 20lb (9kg) and for bitches under 18lb (8kg); for dogs over 20lb (9kg) and for bitches over 18lb (8kg). At Alexandra Palace in

1878 there seemed to be a great interest in size. Classes scheduled then were: Dachshunds, 'Dogs (not exceeding 11in (28cm) high), and 'Bitches (not exceeding 10in (25cm) high). There was the same classification at the Crystal Palace in the same year.

Names registered at about this time were rather interesting; there was 'Bumping Ben', 'Boozing Bob' and 'Castor Legs'. Rather surprisingly the Rev A.T.B. Pinchard called his red bitch 'Queen Victoria', (she was by Maximus out of Ozone, registered in 1888) and Miss Blackoe registered a 'Victoria Regina', who became a champion. In 1900 there was a 'Queen Elizabeth', whose sire was Mephistopeles, and whose colour was described as fawn.

At the Alexandra Palace in 1879 for the first time there was a Champions Class for Dachshunds. The Kennel Club Stud Book of that year carries the following: 'No dog or bitch shall be entitled to be called a Champion that has not won four first prizes at shows registered in the Stud Books, one of the four first prizes being in a Champion Class'; and: 'No dog shall be qualified to compete in a Champion Class that has won less than three prizes'; as well as: 'No dog shall compete in an Open Class that is qualified to compete in a Champions Class, at any show where Champion Classes are provided for that breed.' Those qualifications could be of interest in the show-ring today.

Dapples would seem to have been registered as early as 1876. One bitch, Paulina, born 'about 1876' is described as 'black-and-tan with markings', and she was imported by our Mr Schuller of Poland Street. Mr Healey's Wald'l, bred in Germany by Lieut. Schneider in 1876, was described as 'tan with black markings and spots'. Dapples were firmly established by 1880, and they appear to have been built on the imported dogs, Unser Fritz, Wenzel, Khaki Erdmannsheim and Tiger Reinecke, and at the Alexandra Palace in 1900 there were classes for White, Dappled, Brindle and Piebald, and several shows at about that period included an 'Any Colour' Class.

The First World War caused the collapse of British Dachshunds. Today it seems incredible to recall that Dachshunds were even stoned in the streets, and taunts and insults were hurled at dog and owner alike, so that their owners were frightened to take them out in public. It was perhaps unfortunate for the little Teckel that the Kaiser owned several, and was hardly ever seen in public without them at his heels – even when reviewing his troops, and comic papers and cartoons had made much of this, and so our gallant little Dachshund became a figure of fun, mockery, and even of hatred.

In 1913 the registered number of Dachshunds was 217, but by 1917 the number had fallen to twelve. Yet despite the war 135 shows were held that year, with six of Championship status. Crufts Championship show put on classes for Dachshunds, and the names recorded as having shown were Miss Ethel Dixon (whose prefix was 'Kar'), Mrs Gerald Spencer, Miss M.S. Fanshawe and Mr F.W. Pickering. The judge was Major P.C.G. Hayward.

By 1918 the registration figure had fallen to nine, a year in which no Championship shows were held, and in 1919 no Dachshund was registered. The tide gradually started to turn again, and there were thirty registrations during 1920, and by 1924 the figure had risen to 185.

As can be imagined the state of the breed after the war was in a very sorry state, and very few dogs of quality were left. At this time Major Hayward was Acting Secretary of the Dachshund Club, and he was later to become President; his famous 'Honey' strain had kept going and was to have a marked influence on the breed. Recourse to further importations from Germany were necessary in order to rehabilitate the breed, and in 1923 a Mr Dunlop brought over Theo von Neumarkt and his son, the famous little red, Champion Remagen Max, who was to prove a great benefit to the breed, and to have a great show career.

Between the wars then, a very great number of dogs were imported into Britain, and many were to influence the future type of our breed, and become legends in their day. Many newcomers were attracted to the show-ring, some destined to become household names in the Dachshund world.

The Long-Haired Dachshund

The Long-haired Dachshund was the last of the three types of coat to appear in this country, and they started to arrive round about 1920. At first they appear to have had a struggle to be recognized as Dachshunds; in fact, at a Kennel Club meeting held on 5 March 1929, the Committee decided that Long-haired Dachshunds would have to be classified as 'Any Other Variety, Foreign Dog'. However, a devoted gang of enthusiasts for this beautiful variety of Teckel got together, and in 1930 they formed the Long-haired Daschund Club. After this the long-haired type was recognized by the Kennel Club, and Challenge Certificates were allotted to them. Col. Bedford, Col.

Champion Woodheath Moonlight Sonata by Champion Woodreed Neddie out of Woodheath Golden Lady.

Harrison, Mr Knapp and Mrs Bellamy were some of the great names who worked so hard to achieve this – Col. Bedford imported several dogs from Germany of the 'von Fels' strain, and his famous dog, Champion Otter von Fells, a black-and-tan, became one of the first British Champions. Mrs Bellamy was to breed a string of outstanding champions, and her prefix 'Von Walder', will be found at the back of most pedigrees, as will the lovely 'Primrose Patch' dogs bred by Mrs Smith-Rewse. The pedigree of her Champion Golden Patch, and her Champion Roderick of Primrose Patch who was by Col. Bedford's imported Champion Otter von Fels, will be found in the Appendix.

Colonel Bedford had the great distinction of breeding the first two long-haired champions in 1932. These were Champion Captain of Armadale, who was owned by Mrs Reake, and the bitch Champion Chloe of Armadale, who was owned by Mrs Bellamy.

The early Wire-haired Dachshunds of around this same period after the war were in the capable hands of breeders like Mrs Howard

24

(of the 'Seale' dogs), Mrs Blandy, Air Vice Marshall Sir Charles Lamb, and Miss Theo Watts, to name just a few, and they were largely responsible for the rise in popularity of this attractive variety of Teckel.

Colonel Spurrier and his daughter founded the 'Querns' strain of Smooth-haired Dachshund at about this time, having acquired some of Major Hayward's 'Honey' stock, and Mrs Huggins founded her beautiful 'Firs' strain, which is still revered today. She purchased an imported dog called Friedel von Taubergrund, described as a very smart, active dog, weighing about 17 or 18lb (7.5 or 8kg). It was by in-breeding to him that she produced the first of her long line of Firs champions, as well as by line-breeding to the International Champion Wolf von Birkenschloss, who had been imported from Germany by Madame Rikovsky. Mrs Huggins' Firs Dachshunds were, by today's standards, smallish dogs, but small dogs nevertheless boasting heavy bone and beautiful conformation. The pedigree of Champion Firs Black Velvet, who was to prove one of the great sires of all time, will be found in the Appendix. I am proud to say that the first Dachshund I ever owned was a great grand-daughter of Champion Firs Black Velvet on her dam's side, and a grand-daughter of Champion Max of Buckhurst on her sire's side.

Champion Firs Black Velvet.

The late legendary Madame Rikovsky of immortal Von Der Howitt fame, must surely have imported more great Dachshunds than any other breeder. Madame, as she was always affectionately known to us all, had fled the Russian revolution and, having settled in England, she was to breed and own Dachshunds all her life; and the numerous dogs which she imported from the great kennels in Germany, were to have a profound influence on the breed here in Britain. In 1926 she imported Isolde von Faustenberg and she mated her to Champion Remagen Max, a smallish red import, and this really started the Von Der Howitt strain.

I will mention just a few of her dogs, nearly all of whom will be found way back in the pedigrees of today – International Champion Wolf von Birkenschloss, colour red, imported in 1930, bred by Herr Otto Pohl; Champion Kunz Schneid, colour red, imported in 1937, breeder Herr E. Pohlmey – this little bright red dog was destined to have a great influence on red Dachshunds in this country, and he will be found at the back of most red blood-lines, and even today some of the older breeders talk of 'Schneid red'. Another red dog was the imported Champion Cito von Adlerschroffen, and the beautifully balanced, elegant Gernot von Lindenbuhl, who, to judge from his pictures, would certainly be a great winner today.

Champion Kunz Schneid. Bred in Germany by E. Pohlmey, and imported into Britain by Madame Rikovsky in 1937.

A group of the Adlerschroffen Dachshunds at home in Germany at the time of the importation into Britain of Champion Cito vom Adlerschroffen.

Gernot vom Lindenbuhl. Imported from Germany by Madame Rikovsky.

27

Champion Zeus Vom Schwarenberg – one of the greatest influences on the breed.

There were many more but one of the best was Champion Zeus vom Schwarenberg – a smallish black-and-tan, bred in Germany by Herr Emil Schray, and imported into Britain by Madame Rikovsky just before the Second World War – just in time to make him into a British Champion. This little dog was to have the greatest possible influence on the breed, and he is to be found at the back of nearly all Smooth pedigrees, as well as those of Longs and Wires, both Standard and Miniature. It is interesting to note that he carried a recessive gene for long hair, and long-haired pups were to crop up in litters from time to time. Of course in those days the crossing and inter-breeding of coats and sizes was permitted by the Kennel Club, both here and in Germany, but today puppies bred from mixed parentage cannot be registered in either country. Zeus' pedigree, and that of Champion Kunz Schneid, along with some others is to be found in the Appendix.

Champion Zeus vom Schwarenberg was to sire a great many champions, but his most famous descendant was without doubt his great grandson, Champion Silvae Sailor's Quest, who, despite a very short stud career owing to his tragic early death, sired a great many champion offspring. Quest was bred by Mrs de Caucey Howard, and owned by the Grosvenor Workmans of Silvae fame. Mrs Grosvenor Workman is the President of the Dachshund Club, and her daughter, Jill Johnstone, is still showing the Silvae dogs.

After the war the Silvae Dachshunds were to break all records in most respects, and they had the honour to make up the first post-war Smooth champion in 1946 with Champion Silvae Lustre. Lustre was destined to make history, having the great distinction to be the first ever Dachshund to go Best in Show at an all-breed Championship show. This was the Blackpool Championship Show in 1947, and the judge was the great Mr Marples. Lustre was shown, as always, by Mrs Grosvenor Workman's daughter, Jill. This was indeed a great day for Dachshunds!

The feat was to be repeated in 1954, when Mrs Peggy Hood Wright, of the 'Selwood' Dachshunds, went Best in Show at the Windsor Championship Show, with her chocolate bitch, Champion Selwood Sinderella. The Silvae Dachshunds were to achieve this great honour twice more, with Champion Silvae Post Horn, and Champion Silvae Keeper. For the gallant little Teckel to achieve this was an exciting moment, as usually it is the more striking and glamorous breeds, like Afghans, German Shepherds and so forth, who catch the judge's eye in the final line-up.

More recently the late Bill Pinches, of the Turlshill Dachshunds went Best in Show with his record-breaking chocolate dog, Champion Turlshill Troubadour, and Margaret Swann, of the

Selwood October Lad. Bright red son of Champion Selwood Sailorman who is at the back of many red pedigrees.

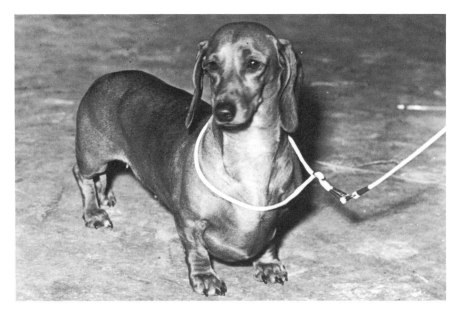

Mr R Pilkington's Champion Ashdown Glamorous. Winner of the Hound group at Crufts in 1953.

Champion Ashdown Pirate. Pirate became a champion in 1954.

Swansford Long-haired Dachshunds recently went Best in Show at the Manchester Championship Show, with Champion Swansford Arrandor, another great record breaker. Jeff Crawford's Champion Voryn's Café au Lait, another Standard Long-hair, went Best in Show at the Hound Show, and Mrs Betty Munt's Champion, Pipersvale Pina-Colada, went Best in Show at the Southern Counties Championship Show, the first Miniature Smooth Dachshund to do so, having won eight Hound Groups at Championship shows. The latest triumph of this nature is the spectacular win of Best in Show at the 1990 Welks Championship show, by Barbara O'Neill's miniature long-haired silver dapple champion, Champion Woodheath Silver Lady, becoming the first Miniature Long-hair to achieve such a victory.

In the post-war years another kennel which came very much to the fore and stamped a type on the breed were the Ashdown Dachshunds, of Mr Bob Pilkington. They were based on Quest and Firs bloodlines, one of their most famous being the great Champion Ashdown Skipper, who was a chocolate-and-tan; but their lovely red bitch, Champion Ashdown Glamorous, made history in 1953

Champion Hawkstone Matelot by Champion Ashdown Skipper out of East Haddon Arabis of Hawkstone. Matelot won over twenty CCs in the 1950s and he was Best in Show at two all-breed championship shows, and at the Great Joint Dachshund Club Championship Show in 1954. He was the sire of a great many champions, both in Britain and overseas.

Champion Moselle von Walder. Miniature Long-haired. By Australian
Champion John of Petersfield out of Miss Cherry of Arundover.

when she won the Hound Group at Crufts, an achievement which
has yet to be repeated by a Dachshund, although a couple have
been Reserve in the Hound Group.

Wire-haired Dachshunds had become numerous enough in
this country by 1929 for the Kennel Club to allocate the first
Challenge Certificates for them, and the long-haired variety got
their first Certificates in 1932.

It was fortunate for the little Teckel that he had become so popular
and so naturalized, that the Second World War did nothing to
diminish his status, unlike those unhappy times in the First World
War. He was accepted everywhere.

After the war, in 1949 both Miniature Long-haired, and Miniature
Smooth-haired were allocated Challenge Certificates, and by 1959,
the last of the six varieties, the Miniature Wire-haired, had also
become numerous enough to be given certificates.

The first Miniature Smooth-haired champions were both awarded
their titles on the same day. They were Mrs E.A. Winders home-
bred red dog, Champion Minivale Miraculous, and Mr Negal's
chocolate bitch, Champion Contessina of Montreux, bred by Mrs
Ivory.

Champion Carmenita of Montreaux – taken when this lovely little bitch was just six months of age. She was to become the smallest bitch champion ever, weighing just 7lb 6oz (3.35kg).

The first Miniature Long-haired champion, made up in 1949, was Champion Marcus of Mornyvarna, owned and bred by Mrs Portman Graham. He was a red dog, and he had actually won a Challenge Certificate competing against Standard Long-hairs, before the varieties had been given separate allocation at shows.

The Miniature Wire-haired Dachshunds were the last of all the varieties to obtain Championship status. A few excellent specimens had been imported by early enthusiasts in the late 1940s from Germany, where they were very popular. Sir Charles Lambe of the Dunkerque wires did much to encourage this delightful variety, and most of the early winners were descended from his Kiwi of Dunkerque, and many of those early winners carried Smooth blood (crossing of the various coats and sizes being permitted in those days).

Championship status was finally achieved in 1959, and the very first Miniature Wire-haired champion was the bitch, Champion Jane of Sillwood, who was owned by Mrs R. Wakefield. The first dog to gain his title was Mrs Muriel Rhodes' Champion Coobeg Ballyteckel Walt Weevil. Looking at the large number and high quality of entries in the show-ring nowadays, it is remarkable how comparatively quickly this little dog has swept to popularity.

Having commented on the fact that the standard of the Dachshund as judged in the show-ring, and the standard of the Dachshund on the Continent differ so widely today, it was apparently not so just before the Second World War. I think it may be of interest to read the report written by the German judge, Dr A.L. Buschkiel after judging the Standard Smooth and the Standard Wire Dachshunds at the 1937 Crufts Coronation Show, where he received a record entry, and judged dogs which have become a legend in the breed. His report was translated by Miss C. van der Meulen, and I quote:

> The shows organized by Mr Charles Cruft already had a great name when I started breeding and exhibiting. They were already world famous when I started judging at larger shows more than 25 years ago. Since then I've judged dogs in many countries, North and South of the equator, but I felt like a 'puppy' when I stood before the organizer of this giant show to thank him for what he has done to make England a second Fatherland for Dachshunds. Though I had only to judge the Smooth and Wire-haired Dachshunds, there were no fewer than

Champion Highlight Von Holzner. Highlight was by Champion
Royce of Nothhanger out of Wyndon Biddy. An early champion in
this variety, and a Crufts winner.

200 dogs (156 Smooth and 44 Wire), and with the many entries I
had to judge a Smooth as many as 297 times, and a Wire 91
times. That's rather a lot, even in two days. Therefore I can
understand quite well that the most patient exhibitors were
afraid I could not finish in time when they saw how much time I
gave even to the last dog. However, I believe that every
exhibitor has got the right to have his dog looked over very
thoroughly. I should have liked to be as thorough in my report,
but my judging book hardly gave any space for remarks; I can't
understand why.

Evidently all a judge has to do is to pick out only a few dogs
and place them; but this was almost impossible, as, on the
whole, the quality was so high. One of the exhibitors remarked
that I seemed to favour light black-and-tans in Smooths; and
light, rather high dogs in Wires. That is not right. I judged from
the point of view that the Dachshund is a working dog who
must be able to move in mountainous as well as in flat country,
without rubbing open his brisket or soon getting tired; he also
has to go to ground after foxes and badgers. The old-fashioned
English show Dachshund could not do this so well, as often
they were rather weak in front, and higher in the quarters than

in front. I eliminated all dogs reminding one of this type, and also all dogs that were too big to go to earth. I was very sorry that in this way some dogs fell out that were correct otherwise; but it is my belief that a judge has the task to show the coming tendency in a breed and to work for its future. I want to state again that in several classes more than twelve dogs could have got the highest qualification 'Excellent', if they had been judged very severely in Germany, as they were almost faultless.

Nearly all the dogs were too fat, which made it very difficult to judge the shoulders and elbows. On the other hand I could see rather quickly which dogs had no muscular toes. An otherwise beautiful bitch struck me as having bad toes as well as being too fat, so she could not get the prize I would have liked to have given her. Competition was so keen that some regular winners did not come into the prizes as they had developed, rather early, a bit of dewlap.

Some young dogs got comparatively low places, as their front legs were too wrinkled. I particularly want to mention this fault. The appearance of some red Dachshunds told me that they descend from a sire who was used very often in Germany for his faultlessly correct shoulders, and his wrinkled front legs have been taken into the bargain. But now it is high time to breed out those wrinkles judicially. There are enough stud dogs for this purpose in England.

On the whole, Great Britain has got sufficient stock to get the small improvements still wanted in the Smooth-haired Dachshund, but it might be good to import from Germany some light, hard stock. Anyhow, the link with the breeding in Germany should not be broken off, as the German Dachshunds are selected continuously for their working capacities. To be as game as a Fox-terrier would be no harm. Then a Dachshund will shrink away from the judge less often when he is being handled. It seemed to me that Wire-haired Dachshunds were better in this respect. I was rather pleased with them, although the general quality was not so high as in the Smooths. Some dogs had decidedly bad fronts and shoulders, and others were too soft in coat. Therefore I put in front those dogs that were exceptionally good in these points. I read a remark that a certain dog I placed second should have been first, but I know quite well why I gave the first prize to the dog with the hardest coat.'

Dr. Buschkiel ends his report with this rather nice paragraph:

'I conclude with whole-hearted thanks to the tireless ring

stewards and the patient exhibitors. Particularly I want to thank the unknown exhibitor, who after the show, asked to thank me for my work, although his dogs had not come into the prizes. This act so impressed me that I won't forget the exhibitors nor the Dachshunds at Cruft's Coronation Dog Show.'

Dr Buschkiel's remark that 'it might be good to import from Germany some light, hard stock' interested me, as surely it was soon after this that Madame Rikovsky was to import the immortal Champion Zeus vom Schwarenberg – perhaps in answer to this plea.

Certainly soon after this time Madame Rikovsky was over in Germany, because she wrote of her impressions of the Dachshunds at the great two-day Championship show held in Munich in April. She noticed that colour was taken into great consideration in the reds, and also the markings in the black-and-tans. The ideal size was much smaller than the English, and what was very noticeable was that ring manners were not studied much: 'Dogs pull at leads and bark to their heart's content, but the judge manages to select what he likes.' She noticed that a kennel which was very successful was the 'vom Schwarenberg'.

I do not think that it is generally realized nowadays how small (compared to our present day Dachshunds), those early imports were. Recently I came across a description of three of Madame Rikovsky's imports which are doubtless way back in all our pedigrees: Champion Wolf vom Birkenschloss (a bright red, weight – 16lb). Gernot vom Lindenbuehl (black-and-tan, weight – under 15lb (6.8kg). And lastly, this report on Champion Cito vom Adlerschroffen 'a red, weighing 16.5lb (7.5kg), only came out of quarantine in the spring of this year, and he became a full Champion within two months'.

Dachshunds in Germany Today

The Dachshund is still one of the most popular dogs in his native homeland, judging from the large registration figures, and from attendance at shows.

As I write this chapter dramatic changes are taking place in Germany, and whereas up till now we have only had accurate figures of registrations and the state of the Teckel in West Germany, now the whole pattern will gradually alter. Dachshunds from what

Postcard bought at Nürnberg station.

Für's **Herrle** !

used to be East Germany will be able now to become registered with the Deutsche Teckelklub, and will be allowed to compete at shows in the west. This is a very happy position, as in the past the Teckel was very highly prized as a pet, and extensively used for sport, in the east.

As these changes are only now beginning to take place, the figures which follow are from West Germany only, although soon these figures will be greatly increased when those from the east are added. The estimated number of Dachshunds registered with the Deutschen Hunde-Verband, an organization similar to our Kennel Club, was 50,000 in 1988, made up of all coats and sizes. The German Teckelklub has its own registration figures, and these are interesting as they reflect the popularity of the different varieties. In 1988 the figures were 15,916 for all coats and sizes; these were made up of 662 Smooth-haired, 11,738 Wire-haired, and 3,516 Long-haired. These figures are for Standard and Miniatures.

There were 331 breed shows held during this same year, and at these breed shows there was an attendance of 8,881 Dachshunds,

Postcard bought at Nürnberg station.

and for all the shows held in 1988 there was an entry of 13,451 Teckels.

The working aspect of the Dachshund is still of the utmost importance in Germany, and field trials and working tests are a regular feature of the life of most Dachshunds in that country. It is estimated that about 4,000 Dachshunds are living and working with the foresters, and apparently about eighty per cent of these Teckels have successfully passed the trial tests. Those who pass successfully are eligible for entry in a separate Stud Book, and qualify for the award of a special working number, which will become part of their name.

The German Teckelklub today has about 28,000 members, and these members will be expected to conform with the rules of membership, and follow the pattern for breeding as laid down by the club.

At the age of eight weeks each litter will be examined by a *Zuchtwart*, a specially appointed breed expert, who will confirm that the pups conform to the breed standard, and any puppy not doing so will be ineligible for registration. He or she then tattoos the puppy on the right ear with six numbers; the first two will indicate the affix (you cannot register without owning an affix), and the

Cover of the 15 July 1958 edition of Der Dachshund, *the official magazine of the German Teckelklub, showing a Wire-haired Dachshund in pursuit of a wounded wild boar.*

40

second two will give the county or region – the last two are the current registration numbers. This tattoo number will be entered on the vaccination certificate, and entered in the Stud Book. A lost Dachshund can therefore be traced to its owner through the Stud Book. A dog or bitch used for breeding must have been first judged 'excellent' or 'very good' at a breed show. No bitch is allowed to be bred from before she is fifteen months old, or after she has passed the age of eight. If you wish to register an unregistered bitch, you can take her to a breed show, and if she is awarded 'excellent' or 'very good', she can then be entered on a special register, but her progeny cannot be entered in the normal Stud Book until the third generation.

As in Britain, no inter-breeding between coats and sizes is permitted today, although in the past, in both countries this was allowed, and we have only to look at the pedigrees of some of the great dogs of days gone by, to see that they carried ancestors of *all* varieties in their lineage.

In Germany the dogs are not weighed, but a chest measurement is taken at the age of fifteen months, which will thereafter be binding, and the dog will then be registered as either Standard, Miniature, or Kaninchenteckel – the three accepted sizes in Germany. The Standard, whose weight is ideally 15–20lb (7–9kg), can have a chest measurement of over 14in (35cm); the Miniature, ideal weight 9lb (4kg), must have a chest measurement which does not exceed 14in (35cm); and lastly the Kaninchenteckel, whose weight should not be above 6.5lb (3kg), should have a chest measurement of approximately 12in (30cm). These measurements will be taken by a judge, and no further measuring or weighing will be necessary.

The German standard is most explicit on the fact that the ground clearance of the dog should be one third of the height (estimated from the withers). This will allow for freedom of movement during work, especially when going to ground.

One of the working tests which the Teckel will undergo consists of a 1,000-metre-long route, over rough terrain, sprinkled with boar blood. After an interval of 40 hours, the handler takes the Dachshund on a six-metre lead, and follows the trail, and at the end of the route the dog will find a little scrap of meat as a reward. The dog will then be judged on his performance – either excellent, very good, or good.

The Teckelklub holds special trials which involve boar, deer, foxes and so forth, and the idea is to find injured game. The Dachshund, on finding the injured prey, is expected to stand with it, and bark, or 'laut', so that the hunter can locate the game. If the dog fails to bark, he fails the test. I imagine that a Teckel discovered wolfing down the remains of a tasty hare would go bottom of the lists for ever!

Underground trials are held, with hares or other game, and again the idea is that once the dog has entered the burrow and located the prey, he must hold it and bark, in order that the hunter can then dig down to it. His function is to hold, not to kill. Another very important test is to make sure that the dog is not gun-shy. At this trial, two shots are fired over the dog – he should ignore them, and stand his ground. If he should fail to do so, he or she will not be allowed to compete in any further working trials.

Until the demolition of the Berlin Wall, only working stock in East Germany, (dogs working with the foresters), were permitted to be registered, or to be bred from, and their breeding programme was heavily supervised. Now, happily all this is in the process of change. The German Teckelklub is making contact with the authorities in the east, exchanging ideas, and will allow eventual registration with the club, and mutual attendance at shows, both in the west and the east.

Dachshunds in the United States

The Dachshund was becoming popular in the United States from as early as the mid-nineteenth century, as indeed it was in Britain. Many in America were doubtless brought over by German immigrants, and indeed some came from illustrious kennels. Two of the very earliest imports we hear about are Caesar and Minka, who were both black-and-tan, and they were used with success by their owner, Mr Fleischmann to hunt woodchucks in the mountains. However it was not until 1879 that the first Dachshunds were actually registered, and the Dachshund Club of America was founded when it was recognized by the American Kennel Club in 1895, its first President being Mr Harry Peters.

In those very early days Dachshunds were strong in the west, and in the years immediately preceeding the First World War the Western Dachshund Club had many enthusiastic members, several being themselves of German descent, and they imported many dogs from Germany.

Sadly, as in Britain, the First World War caused havoc among

Dachshund owners in America, as everything German was liable to be persecuted. It is said that during this terrible period one member of the Western Dachshund Club went out to his kennels and shot every one of his Dachshunds. During this war the name Dachshund was dropped, and for a few years the title Badger Hound replaced it. Happily in 1923 the name Dachshund was restored to the breed, to the clubs, and the catalogues.

After the war the Dachshund continued to rise in popularity, and it is during this period that the many famous imports into America took place. It strikes me as extremely interesting that so many of these imports came from the same kennels as numerous British imports of the same period. Names which stand out are Asbecks, Luitpoldsheims, Lichtensteins, Marienlusts, Von Falltors and many more. So it is safe to say that British and American Dachshunds have the same ancestry. Imports were made from Britain into America as well, with great success. In fact the first Dachshund ever to go Best in Show all breeds in the United States was an English import – Champion Kensal Call Boy.

Specialist shows were held from 1935 onwards with enormous entries, and the number of Dachshunds registered by the American Kennel Club has continued to rise ever since, and today the Dachshund is very high numerically on the list of all breeds.

Fortunately, by the time of the Second World War the Dachshund had become so naturalized that there was never any question of persecution, and he continued to rise in popularity.

The standard of the Dachshund as drawn up by both the British Kennel Club and the American Kennel Club has been largely adapted from the original German breed standard, and they are very similar (the standards of both are fully reproduced in Chapter 2). Indeed we are still able to exchange judges between our countries, and there are regular and very happy exchanges on both sides, and we continue to import and export each other's bloodlines.

The Dachshund Club of America produces a most useful newsletter each month, filled with interesting articles, photographs of current winners, and so forth. In that huge country there are a great many regional Dachshund Clubs, all holding specialist shows, field trials and producing newsletters. Most Clubs seem to run obedience classes, and the Dachshund Club of America has a very active field trial programme. Some of these trials are purely for fun, others are graded, and both members and judges are instructed at seminars held around the country.

The method for making up a champion differs in the States from that in Britain. Britain asks for a dog to have been awarded three Challenge Certificates by three different judges before he is entitled to that coveted title. In the States, however, they run a rather complicated 'points' system. Fifteen points are required for the Champion title. The most points available at any one show is five, so at the very best a dog must win at three different shows. However it is not quite as simple as that, as the points that are available vary from area to area, and they are also allocated according to how many dogs are entered.

In South Africa incidentally, where I started my show career, Challenge Certificates were awarded, as in Britain, but in order to gain the title of champion we had to win four Challenge Certificates under three different judges, and in three different provinces. For instance you could get two in the Cape, but you had to travel to, say, Natal, Transvaal or Free State for the others.

As we see from the official American standard there is no mention made of any weight limit or recommended weight. Miniatures must in general compete with standards, excepting for a special class of 'Under 10lb', so for that big award of points, a miniature will have to hold his own and beat his larger brother. In the booklet *Guidelines for Dog Show Judges*, printed by the American Kennel Club we read:

> In any breed where certain weights are specified as disqualifications, or in any class or division the conditions of which include a weight specification, judges are responsible for having a dog weighed if they suspect it is not within the limits. If a dog is weighed and found to be ineligible for its class or division, the judge must excuse the dog, marking the judge's book 'Excused, ineligible, weighed out'. Such a dog cannot be disqualified unless the weight requires disqualification under the breed standard. Any dog declared ineligible cannot be transferred to another class or division at the show or at any subsequent show for which entries have already closed. No dog whose breed standard does not include a weight disqualification or that is not competing in a class or division with a weight specification may be weighed.

The classification for Dachshunds at all dog shows in America, held under Kennel Club rules, is just three – Long-haired, Smooth and Wire-haired, as opposed to the classification in Britain of six varieties – Standard Long-haired, Smooth and Wire-haired, and Miniature Long-haired, Smooth and Wire-haired.

2

The Standard

The revised standard for the Hound Group, which of course includes all six varieties of Dachshunds, was published by the Kennel Club in 1986, and is as follows:

The British Breed Standard (Reproduced by kind permission of the Kennel Club of Great Britain)

General Appearance

Long and low, but with compact, well muscled body, bold defiant carriage of head and intelligent expression.

Characteristics

Intelligent, lively, courageous to the point of rashness, obedient. Especially suited to going to ground because of low build, very strong forequarters, and forelegs, long strong jaw, and immense power of bite and hold. Excellent nose, persevering hunter and tracker.

Temperament

Faithful, versatile and good tempered.

Head and Skull

Long, appearing conical when seen from above; from side tapering uniformly to tip of nose. Skull only slightly arched. Neither too broad nor too narrow, sloping gradually without prominent stop into slightly arched muzzle. Length from tip of nose to eyes equal to length from eyes to occiput. In Wire haired, particularly, ridges over

45

Champion Frankenwen Gold Braid. Red bitch by Mandarin of Phaeland out of Champion Frankenwen Gold Bangle. She had a wonderful show record as a puppy and now has already won ten CCs and two hound groups and has been Best in Show at the Dachshund Club Championship Show. Her litter sister, Frankenwen Gold Brocade is also a champion.

eyes strongly prominent, giving appearance of slightly broader skull. Lips well stretched, neatly covering lower jaw. Strong jaw bones not too square or snipey, but opening wide.

Eyes

Medium size, almond shaped, set obliquely. Dark except in Chocolates, where they can be lighter. In Dapples one or both 'Wall' eyes permissible.

Ears

Set high, and not too far forward. Broad, of moderate length, and well rounded (not pointed or folded). Forward edge touching cheek. Mobile, and when at attention back of ear directed forward and outward.

Champion Womack Wrightstarturn. Wrightstarturn had a wonderful show career, and was the sire of six champions.

Two good heads – Deepfurrows Romeo and Deepfurrows Sky Princess.

Mouth

Teeth strongly developed, powerful canine teeth fitting closely. Jaws strong, with a perfect, regular and complete scissor bite, i.e. the upper teeth closely overlapping the lower teeth and set square to jaws. Complete dentition important.

Neck

Long muscular, clean with no dewlap, slightly arched, running in graceful lines into shoulders, carried proudly forward.

Forequarters

Shoulder blades long, broad, and placed firmly and obliquely (45 degrees to the horizontal) upon very robust rib cage. Upper arm the same length as shoulder blade, set at 90 degrees to it, very strong and covered with hard, supple muscles. Upper arm lies close to ribs, but able to move freely. Forearm short and strong in bone, inclining slightly inwards; when seen in profile moderately straight, must not bend forward or knuckle over, which indicates unsoundness. Correctly placed foreleg should cover lowest point of the keel.

Body

Long and full muscled. Back level, with sloping shoulders, lying in straightest possible line between withers and slightly arched loin. Loin short and strong. Breast bone strong, and so prominent that a depression appears on either side of it in front. When viewed from front, thorax full and oval; when viewed from side or above, full volumed, so allowing by its ample capacity complete development of heart and lungs. Well ribbed up, underline gradually merging into line of abdomen. Body sufficiently clear of ground to allow free movement.

Hindquarters

Rump full, broad and strong, pliant muscles. Croup long, full, robustly muscled, only slightly sloping towards tail. Pelvis strong, set obliquely and not too short. Upper thigh set at right angles to pelvis, strong and of good length. Lower thigh short, set at right

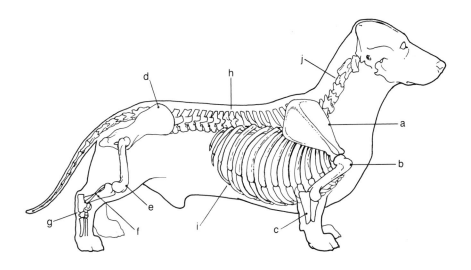

(a) shoulder blade. (b) upper arm (humerus). (c) forearm (ulna).
(d) pelvis. (e) femur. (f) tibia and fibula. (g) tarsus. (h) vertebrae.
(i) ribcage. (j) neck bones. (cervical vertebrae).

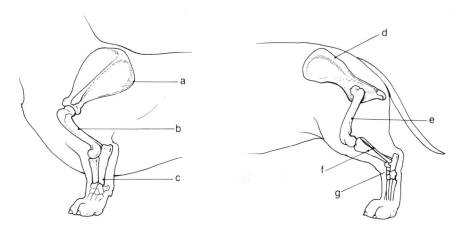

(a) shoulder blade. (b) upper arm (humerus). (c) forearm (ulna).
(d) pelvis. (e) femur. (f) tibia and fibula. (g) tarsus.

49

Champion Rhinefields Amala by Champion Descendent of Rhinefields out of Champion Rhinefields Amapola. In her show career Amala broke all records for Standard Smooth Dachshunds winning fifty-two Challenge Certificates under different judges.

angles to upper thigh and well muscled. Legs when seen behind, set well apart, straight, and parallel. Hind dew claws undesirable.

Feet

Front feet full, broad, deep, close knit, straight or very slightly turned out. Hind feet smaller and narrower. Toes close together, with a decided arch to each toe, strong regularly placed nails, thick and firm pads. Dog must stand true, i.e. equally on all parts of the foot.

Tail

Continues line of spine, but slightly curved, without kinks or twists, not carried too high, or touching ground when at rest.

50

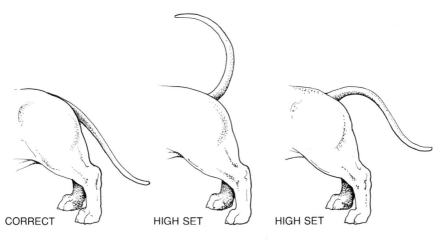

CORRECT   HIGH SET   HIGH SET

Tails.

Gait/Movement

Should be free and flowing. Stride should be long, with the drive coming from the hindquarters when viewed from the side. Viewed from in front or behind, the legs and feet should move parallel to each other with the distance apart being the width of the shoulder and hip joints respectively.

Coat

Smooth-Haired Dense, short and smooth. Hair on underside of tail coarse in texture. Skin loose and supple, but fitting closely all over without dewlap and little or no wrinkle.

Long-Haired Soft and straight, or only slightly waved; longest under neck, on underparts of body, and behind legs, where it forms abundant feathering, on tail where it forms a flag. Outside of ears well feathered. Coat flat, and not obscuring outline. Too much hair on feet undesirable.

Wire-Haired With exception of jaw, eyebrows, chin and ears, the whole body should be covered with a short, harsh coat with dense undercoat, beard on the chin, eyebrows bushy, but hair on ears almost smooth. Legs and feet well but neatly furnished with harsh coat.

51

Champion Andlouis' Black Knight. Standard Wire-haired brindle dog. By Champion Quitrutec Homeward Bound out of Andlouis' Golden Topaz. Black Knight had already won twenty-one CCs and nineteen Best of Breeds before the age of three, as well as the hound group at the Ladies Kennel Association.

Champion Drakesleat Ai Jail by Champion Drakesleat Dick Darstardly, out of Champion Drakesleat Kalamity Kate. She was top Miniature Wire for four years, and the record is now held by her daughter, Champion Drakesleat Ai Jinks.

Colour

All colours allowed but (except in Dapples which should be evenly marked all over) no white permissible, save for a small patch on chest which is permitted but not desirable. Nose and nails black in all colours except chocolate/tan and chocolate/dapple, where brown permitted.

Weight and Size

Standards   Ideal weight 20–26lb (9–12kg).

Miniatures   Ideal weight 10lb (4.5kg). It is of the utmost importance that judges should not award prizes to animals over 11lb (5kg).

Faults

Any departure from the foregoing points should be considered a fault and the seriousness with which the fault should be regarded should be in exact proportion to its degree.

Note

Male animals should have two apparently normal testicles fully descended into the scrotum.

Before discussing some sections of the standard more fully, it might be of interest to remember that the original British standard was adopted, fairly faithfully, from the German standard, which differs only in so much as it is much more detailed on every count, and that this standard was drawn up with reference to the fact that the Teckel was very much a working dog, created for a specific purpose, or purposes, and that each aspect of the standard had these functions very much in mind.

To take one small example, the standard penalizes too much dewlap. In the early German standard this was described as undesirable because it was 'fuchsfutter', or fox food, implying that the unfortunate dog could be seized by the loose skin by his quarry.

I know that in Britain today the Dachshund is no longer required to work against any of his traditional enemies, but we love this gallant little dog for all those characteristics which, for generations,

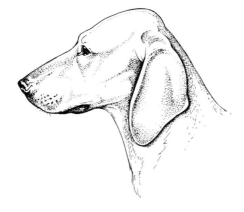

a

b

(a) correct outline. (b) correct head.

were bred into him, so we should endeavour to respect them, and to keep them alive.

The first characteristic in the standard of long and low is self-explanatory, but it should be borne in mind that lowness means lowness from the withers, *not* lack of ground clearance. A dog moving over snow, rough ground and so forth, could be seriously impeded by being too low, and a bitch heavily in whelp could become almost incapable of moving without damaging her teats.

Strong forequarters are so important to the burrowing dog – strong jaws and immense power of bite and hold are perhaps one of

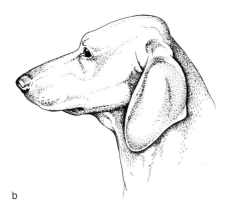

(a) *Poor outline, tucked up and forward in the shoulder.*
(b) *Poor head, too much stop, throaty and snipey jaw.*

the most important working points, because the Dachshund, although a small dog, possesses a really powerful jaw and teeth for his size which can hold on to almost anything when aroused. His tremendous scenting ability is a fact which has surprised many an obedience trainer, and when he cares to use it the Teckel has a nose second to none.

Anyone who has ever owned a Dachshund will vouch for that faithfulness of temperament, one of the greatest reasons why we all love him, and we *must* maintain it in our lovely breed.

The head, the eyes and the ears are very important as they are in fact the first things we see when looking at a Dachshund. The expression should be lively, but kind. Dark eyes are important with the darker coats, as pale eyes give a 'foxy', untrustworthy appearance, except in the Dapples and Chocolates, but even then a darker eye is much more attractive. Too round eyes are a fault. The eyes should be as stated, almond-shaped, yet many today, even in our champions, are too round.

Ugly, high-set ears can completely spoil the appearance, as can too pendulous or low-set ears. The art of recognizing a good, correctly proportioned head is greatly helped by studying the heads of winning dogs, either from illustrations and photographs, or from attending breed shows. If you are a novice and own a Dachshund with a poor head, it is likely that you will think that this is the correct type, and you will have to work hard to recognize the right type. A too-broad skull can give a beagle-like look to the dog, and a snipey jaw can mean that the dog will lack that vital strength and ability to grab and hold his prey.

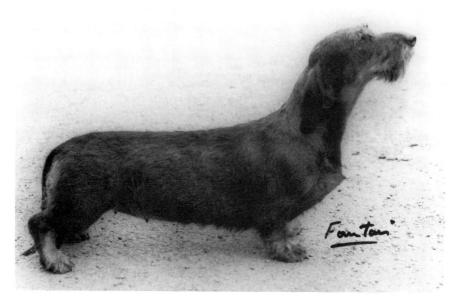

Champion Tan Trudi of Thornton. Wire-haired brindle bitch by Champion Mordax Music Master out of Rheinhessia of Appletrees. Trudi won eighteen CCs and thirteen Best of Breeds and the Dunkerque Trophy in 1974.

Head study of a Standard Wire-haired Dachshund.

English and Irish Champion Wingcrest Smart Alec. This little black-and-tan Miniature Smooth obtained his title at 15½ months of age and he has since won twenty-nine CCs and has sired many champions. He has been top dog in his breed for three years.

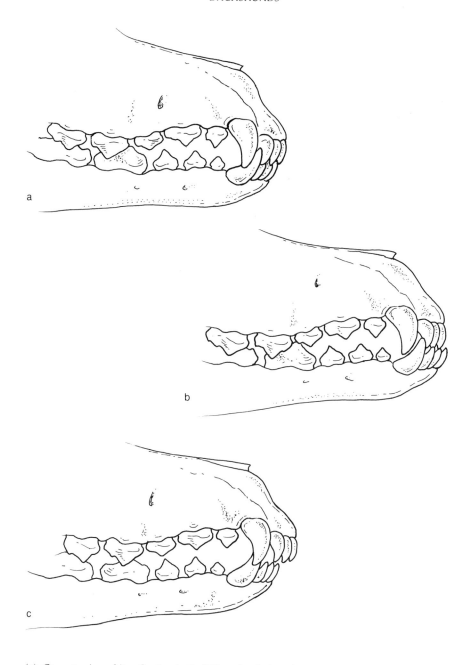

(a) *Correct scissor bite. Canine teeth fitting closely together.*
(b) *Incorrect bite. The lower jaw jutting forward – undershot.*
(c) *Incorrect bite. The upper jaw jutting forward – overshot.*

It is very important that the strong teeth fit closely into the correct scissor bite, and that they are neither undershot (inferior protusion), or overshot (superior protusion). At one time a pincer bite (the teeth meeting exactly edge to edge), was permitted on the continent, it being believed that such a bite was more capable of hanging on to prey, but today, on the continent as well as in Britain, it is considered a fault, and only the scissor bite is recognized as correct.

In very young puppies it is important to examine the mouth, when all the milk teeth are present, at about six weeks old, and if at *this* stage the bite is a correct scissors bite, it is virtually certain that when the permanent teeth come through, at between four to five months, that they will be correct. However it is useful to remember that in the dog, as in humans, the lower jaw grows more slowly than the upper jaw (you have only to look at young children to confirm this), and there can be a stage when the pup, at round about five months, appears to be overshot. Keep a check on the mouth, as most often, if the fault is only slight, you find that the lower jaw catches up with the upper. Should the reverse happen, and the pup, either in the nest or when the permanent teeth start to erupt, be undershot, my advice would be to sell it as a pet, possibly without papers so that it cannot be bred from, as this fault will never correct itself, and it is important to eradicate it from any breeding programme.

lower teeth 22

upper teeth 20

*Champion Yatesbury Big Bang, by Champion Landmark Witch
Doctor out of Champion Yatesbury Nanette. His two litter brothers
are also champions.*

A long neck is very attractive, especially in a show dog. A dog
who carries his head proudly when being exhibited is on the way to
winning. The long, reachy neck was considered useful when the
dog was working underground, enabling him to reach forward to
grab his quarry. Correct shoulder placement, with upper arm tight
to a rounded rib cage is very important – it means that the dog will
move correctly and loose shoulders breed loose movement.

The body should be long, but should appear in proportion. The
back should appear level, but flexible, with a very slight rise over the
loins. The prominent chest is a particular feature of the Dachshund,
and allows for heart and lung room, which is so important when
working. There is a great danger in this respect of exaggeration, and
some breeders, and indeed some judges, consider that if a
prominent chest and deep keel is required, the bigger the better,
although an unbalanced dog is the result. Balance and harmony
should be the aim. The breast bone, or sternum, should be
prominent. The whole chest or keel, viewed from the side,
appearing like the prow of a ship.

The hindquarters, which are of paramount importance to the
correct gait of the dog, are far too often too light and narrow. The

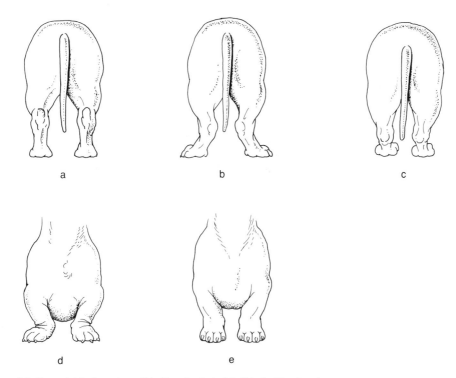

(a) Correct hindquarters. (b) Cow-hocked. (c) Weak, Toe-ing in.
(d) Incorrect front, weak, and showing wrinkle. (e) Correct front.

Dachshund is a small dog, but for his size he should have really heavy bone, and this should be apparent in the hindquarters as well as the front. The rump should be nicely muscled and round. The hind feet are less rounded and full than the front feet. The front feet should have that fat, cat-like appearance ideally, with nicely arched toes and full pads.

The standard states that the movement of the dog should be free and flowing. The hind legs must be true when moving, not knuckling in or going too wide. In so many cases when seen going away the dog appears to 'throw a leg', i.e. it turns inwards, and in consequence the animal would become unsound when fully exercised. When going away the hindquarters should show straight parallel action, and the legs should be lifted smartly and clear the ground. The front appearance of the dog when approaching will show that the shoulders and feet remain parallel, and that the elbows are tight and do not stick out. The weight should fall

61

correctly on each front leg, and should you be able to follow the tracks made by a sound Dachshund, for example in snow, because the imprints of the hind legs would follow in a straight line with the front ones.

The coat of the Dachshund is one of its many glories. A good smooth coat should need little or no attention, save an occasional brushing, being dense, strong and shining in appearance. Wrinkle, as stated in the standard is an undesirable fault. In Wires the appearance from a distance should be almost that of a Smooth. The coat should be dense and harsh, with a thick undercoat. Soft, fluffy coats, although they can look attractive, are incorrect, and they can be a source of endless grooming, and really should be avoided. A Wire Dachshund should have a wire coat. That these problems exist in their variety is no doubt due to the introduction, in the early days, of the various crosses. The soft coat for instance goes back to the Dandie Dinmont, whereas the miniature Schnauzer cross gave a good harsh coat.

The beautiful coat of the long-haired variety is indeed its crowning glory. The coat should be straight, as the standard states,

Champion Woodheath Silver Brocade. Miniature Long-haired, beautifully marked silver dapple bitch, by Forestway Great Expectations out of Woodheath Silver Sequin.

Beautiful head of the Miniature Long-haired bitch, Champion Woodheath Cluanie of Tuonela.

and only slightly waved – it is true to say that today far too many coats are heavy and too profuse. The long-hair used to be particularly prized as a water dog, but I imagine that many today would become waterlogged and sink without trace, if used for this.

The size of the Miniatures is self-explanatory. Sadly the limit of 11lb (5kg) can lead to very thin and starved-looking animals being exhibited, and there has been some lobbying for an increase in the weight limit. In Germany, as we have seen, the Miniatures are only weighed once in their career.

The ideal weight quoted for a Standard of 20–26lb (9–12kg) is a perennial subject for discussion. It is however, a *recommendation* only, and until the day when scales are present in the ring, as is the case with the Miniatures, weight is a matter left to the discretion of the judge. It is a sad fact that a great many of the winning exhibits in the ring today, in the Standard Smooths especially, weigh well over 26lb (12kg). If breeders weigh their own dogs, they are well aware of this. The result is that if a smaller dog, say one who weighs around 23 or 24lb (10.5–11kg) appears in the ring, he stands less chance of winning against the bigger, more impressive looking rivals. This is all wrong. A dog who was bred to go to ground would not be able to do so were he too large.

One of the best dogs, in my opinion, that I bred, weighed 23lb (10.5kg), but after puppyhood was seldom placed highly as he was considered too small. Yet in the pre-war days, all the great Firs Champions of Mrs Basil Huggins, so typical of the ideal, with grand chests, deep keels and heavy bone and quarters, weighed around 18–23lb (8–10.5kg). Here again it is up to the judge. It would be a great pity if the breed were to become too coarse and heavy. 'Exaggeration,' say the Chinese, 'is to draw a snake, and add legs.'

The Original Standard

Before ending this chapter on the standard, I think it might be of interest to have a look at the original standard, and at the points value given to some features.

Champion Pipersvale Pina-Colada by Champion Monksmile Dan-de-Lion out of Champion Pipersvale Beaujolais. 'Oliver' has won seventy Challenge Certificates during his show career, and he won Best in Show at the Southern Counties Championship, thus becoming the first Miniature Smooth to go Best in Show at an all breed championship show.

The Dachshund Standard, as Settled by the Dachshund Club (November, 1881)

Head and Skull   Long, level and narrow; peak, well developed, no stop; eyes intelligent and somewhat small; follow body in colour.   12

Ears   Long, broad, and soft; set on low and well back; carried close to the head. $6\frac{1}{2}$

Jaw   Strong, level, and square to the muzzle; canines recurvent.   5

Chest   Deep and narrow; breast bone prominent.   7

Legs and Feet   Fore-legs very short and strong in bone, well crooked, not standing over; elbows well clothed with muscle, neither in nor out; feet large, round and strong, with thick pads and strong nails. Hind legs smaller in bone and higher, hind feet smaller. The dog must stand true, i.e. equally on all parts of the foot.   20

Skin and Coat   Skin thick, loose, supple, and in great quantity; coat dense, short and strong.   13

Loin   Well arched, long, and muscular.   8

Stern   Long and strong, flat at root, tapering to the tip; hair on underside coarse; carried low, except when excited. Quarters very muscular.   5

Body   Length from back of head to root of stern, $2\frac{1}{2}$ times the height at shoulder. Fore-ribs well sprung, back ribs very short. $8\frac{1}{2}$

Colour   Any colour, nose to follow body colour; much white objectionable.   4

Symmetry and Quality   The Dachshund should be long, low and graceful, not cloddy.   11

—

Total   100

Weight   Dogs about 21lb; bitches about 18lb.

The Dachshund Club do not advocate point judging; the figures are only used to show the comparative value of the features.

The Official Standard for the Dachshund, as published by the American Kennel Club is reproduced below. It is very similar to that of the British Standard, and as they both were adapted from the original German standard in the first place, it is not very surprising that they are so alike. The American Standard is very much more detailed, and yet differs from the British on several points. For instance in the standard there is no mention made of male animals having, as described in the British Standard, 'two apparently normal testicles fully descended in the scrotum'. In another publication, entitled *Guidelines for Dog Show Judges*, it is mentioned under a section entitled 'Disqualifying Faults'.

In the British standard all coats and sizes are required to have the same construction, yet in the American standard under the section (2) Wirehaired Dachshund, it states: 'The general appearance is the same as that of the shorthaired, but without being long in the legs, it is permissible for the body to be somewhat higher off the ground.'

There is also no mention made of weight requirements for Standards *or* for Miniatures, except that they are permitted to enter a special class for 'under 10 pounds and 12 months old or over'.

Another slight variation between the two Standards is with reference to the eyes. In the British standard it states: 'In Dapples one or both "Wall" eyes permissible', whereas in the American Standard we read: 'Wall eyes in the case of dapple dogs are not a very bad fault, but are also not desirable.'

The American Breed Standard
(Reproduced by kind permission of the
American Kennel Club)

General Features

General Appearance Low to ground, short-legged, long-bodied, but with compact figure and robust muscular development; with bold and confident carriage of the head and intelligent facial expression. In spite of his shortness of leg, in comparison with his length of trunk, he should appear neither crippled, awkward, cramped in his capacity for movement, nor slim and weasel-like.

Qualities He should be clever, lively, and courageous to the point of rashness, persevering in his work both above and below ground; with all the senses well developed. His build and disposition qualify him especially for hunting game below ground. Added to this, his hunting spirit, good nose, loud tongue, and small size, render him especially suited for beating the bush. His figure and his fine nose give him an especial advantage over most other breeds of sporting dogs for trailing.

Head study of Mrs Andrews Miniature Wire-haired Champion Drakesleat Dick Dastardly. Sire of many champions and top stud dog in 1977 and 1978.

Conformation of Body

Head Viewed from above or from the side, it should taper uniformly to the tip of the nose, and should be clean-cut. The skull is only slightly arched, and should slope gradually without stop (the less stop the more typical) into the finely-formed slightly-arched muzzle (ram's nose). The bridge bones over the eyes should be strongly prominent. The nasal cartilage and tip of the nose are long and narrow; lips tightly stretched, well covering the lower jaw, but neither deep nor pointed; corner of the mouth not very marked. Nostrils well open. Jaws opening wide and hinged well back of the eyes, with strongly developed bones and teeth.

Teeth Powerful canine teeth should fit closely together, and the outer side of the lower incisors should tightly touch the inner side of the upper. (Scissors bite.)

Eyes Medium size, oval, situated at the sides, with a clean, energetic, though pleasant expression; not piercing. Colour, lustrous dark reddish-brown to brownish-black for all coats and colours. Wall eyes in the case of dapple dogs are not a very bad fault, but are also not desirable.

Ears Should be set near the top of the head, and not too far forward, long but not too long, beautifully rounded, not narrow,

67

pointed, or folded. Their carriage should be animated, and the forward edge should just touch the cheek.

Neck   Fairly long, muscular, clean-cut, not showing any dewlap on the throat, slightly arched in the nape, extending in a graceful line into the shoulders, carried proudly but not stiffly.

Front   To endure the arduous exertion underground, the front must be correspondingly muscular, compact, deep, long and broad.

Forequarters in detail:

Shoulder Blade   Long, broad, obliquely and firmly placed upon the fully developed thorax, finished with hard and plastic muscles.

Upper Arm   Of the same length as the shoulder blade, and at right angles to the latter, strong of bone and hard of muscle, lying close to the ribs, capable of free movement.

Forearm   This is short in comparison to other breeds, slightly turned inwards; supplied with hard but plastic muscles on the front and outside, with tightly stretched tendons on the inside and at the back.

Joint between forearm and foot (wrists)   These are closer together than the shoulder joints, so that the front does not appear absolutely straight.

Paws   Full, broad in front, and a trifle inclined outwards; compact, with well-arched toes and tough pads.

Toes   There are five of these, though only four are in use. They should be close together, with a pronounced arch; provided on top with strong nails, and underneath with tough toe-pads. Dewclaws may be removed.

Trunk   The whole trunk should in general be long and fully muscled. The back, with sloping shoulders, and short, rigid pelvis, should lie in the straightest possible line between the withers and the very slightly arched loins, these latter being short, rigid, and broad.

Chest   The breastbone should be strong, and so prominent in front that on either side a depression (dimple) appears. When viewed from the front, the thorax should appear oval, and should extend downward to the mid-point of the forearm. The enclosing structure of ribs should appear full and oval, and when viewed from above or from the side, full-volumed, so as to allow by its ample capacity, complete development of heart and lungs. Well-ribbed up, and gradually merging into the line of the abdomen. If the length is

68

correct, and also the anatomy of the shoulder and upper arm, the front legs when viewed in profile should cover the lowest point of the breast line.

Abdomen Slightly drawn up.

Hindquarters The hindquarters viewed from behind should be of completely equal width.

Croup Long, round, full, robustly muscled, but plastic; only slightly sinking toward the tail.

Pelvic Bones Not too short, rather strongly developed, and moderately sloping.

Thigh Bone Robust and of good length, set at right angles to the pelvic bones.

Hind Legs Robust and well-muscled, with well-rounded buttocks.

Knee Joint Broad and strong.

Calf Bone In comparison with other breeds, short; it should be perpendicular to the thigh bone, and firmly muscled.

The bones at the base of the foot (tarsus) Should present a flat appearance, with a strongly prominent hock and a broad tendon of Achilles.

The central foot bones (metatarsus) Should be long, movable toward the calf bone, slightly bent toward the front, but perpendicular (as viewed from behind).

Hind Paws Four compactly closed and beautifully arched toes, as in the case of the front paws. The whole foot should be posed equally on the ball and not merely on the toes; nails short.

Tail Set in continuation of the spine, extending without very pronounced curvature, and should not be carried too gaily.

Note Inasmuch as the Dachshund is a hunting dog, scars from honourable wounds shall not be considered a fault.

Special Characteristics of the Three Coat Varieties

The Dachshund is bred with three varieties of coat: (1) Shorthaired (or Smooth); (2) Wirehaired; (3) Longhaired. All three varieties should conform to the characteristics already specified. The long-haired and shorthaired are old, well-fixed varieties, but into the wirehaired Dachshund, the blood of other breeds has been purposely introduced; nevertheless, in breeding him, the greatest

Champion Ralines Maid To Measure, by Champion Darisca D'vere out of Ralines Helen of Troy. Top winning bitch in the breed for 1988, 1989 and 1990.

stress must be placed upon conformity to the general Dachshund type. The following specifications are applicable separately to the three coat-varieties, respectively:

(1) Shorthaired (or Smooth) Dachshund

Hair Short, thick, smooth and shining; no bald patches. Special faults are: too fine or thin hair, leathery ears, bald patches, too coarse or too thick hair in general.

Tail Gradually tapered to a point, well but not too richly haired, long, sleek bristles on the underside are considered a patch of strong-growing hair, not a fault. A brush tail is a fault, as is also a partly or wholly hairless tail.

Color of Hair, Nose and Nails:
One-Colored Dachshund This group includes red (often called tan), red-yellow, yellow, and brindle, with or without a shading of interspersed black hairs. Nevertheless a clean color is preferable,

and red is to be considered more desirable than red-yellow or yellow. Dogs strongly shaded with interspersed black hairs belong to this class, and not to the other color groups. A small white spot is admissible, but not desirable. Nose and Nails – Black; brown is admissible, but not desirable.

Two-Colored Dachshund These comprise deep black, chocolate, grey (blue), and white; each with tan markings over the eyes, on the sides of the jaw and underlip, on the inner edge of the ear, front, breast, inside and behind the front legs, on the paws and around the anus, and from there to about one-third to one-half of the length of the tail on the under side. The most common two-colored Dachshund is usually called black-and-tan. A small white spot is admissible but not desirable. Absence, undue prominence or extreme lightness of tan markings is undesirable. Nose and Nails – In the case of black dogs, black; for chocolate, brown (the darker the better); for grey (blue) or white dogs, grey or even flesh color, but the last named color is not desirable; in the case of white dogs, black nose and nails are to be preferred.

Champion Hobbithill Zephania. Miniature Smooth by Champion Braishvale Jumping Jack out of Hobbithill Polly.

Dappled Dachshund The color of the dappled Dachshund is a clear brownish or greyish color, or even a white ground, with dark irregular patches of dark-grey, brown, red-yellow or black (large areas of one color not desirable). It is desirable that neither the light nor the dark color should predominate. Nose and Nails – As for One-and Two-Colored Dachshund.

(2) Wirehaired Dachshund

The general appearance is the same as that of the short-haired, but without being long in the legs, it is permissible for the body to be somewhat higher off the ground.

Hair With the exception of jaw, eyebrows, and ears, the whole body is covered with a perfectly uniform tight, short, thick, rough, hard coat, but with finer, shorter hairs (undercoat) everywhere distributed between the coarser hairs, resembling the coat of the German Wirehaired Pointer. There should be a beard on the chin. The eyebrows are bushy. On the ears the hair is shorter than on the body; almost smooth, but in any case conforming to the rest of the coat. The general arrangement of the hair should be such that the wirehaired Dachshund, when seen from a distance should resemble the smooth-haired. Any sort of soft hair in the coat is faulty, whether short or long, or wherever found on the body; the same is true of long, curly, or wavy hair, or hair that sticks out irregularly in all directions; a flag tail is also objectionable.

Tail Robust, as thickly haired as possible, gradually coming to a point, and without a tuft.

Color of Hair, Nose and Nails All colors are admissible. White patches on the chest, though allowable, are not desirable.

(3) Longhaired Dachshund

The distinctive characteristic differentiating this coat from the short-haired, or smooth-haired Dachshund is alone the rather long silky hair.

Hair The soft, sleek, glistening, often slightly wavy hair should be longer under the neck, on the underside of the body, and especially on the ears and behind the legs, becoming there a pronounced feather; the hair should attain its greatest length on the underside of the tail. The hair should fall beyond the lower edge of the ear. Short hair on the ear, so-called 'leather' ears, is not desirable. Too luxurious a coat causes the longhaired Dachshund to seem coarse, and masks the type. The coat should remind one of the Irish Setter, and should give the dog an elegant appearance. Too thick hair on the paws, so-called 'mops', is inelegant, and renders the animal unfit for use. It is faulty for the dog to have equally long hair over all the body, if the coat is too curly, or too scrubby, or if a flag tail or overhanging hair on the ears are lacking; or if there is a very pronounced parting on the back, or a vigorous growth between the toes.

Tail Carried gracefully in prolongation of the spine; the hair attains here its greatest length and forms a veritable flag.

Color of Hair, Nose and Nails Exactly as for the smooth-haired Dachshund, except that the red-with-black (heavily sabled) color is permissible and is formally classed as a red.

Miniature Dachshunds

Note Miniature Dachshunds are bred in all three coats. Within the limits imposed, symmetrical adherence to the general Dachshund conformation, combined with smallness, and mental and physical vitality, should be the outstanding characteristics of Miniature Dachshunds. They have not been given separate classification but are a division of the Open Class for 'under 10 pounds, and 12 months old or over.'

General Faults

Serious Faults Over- or undershot jaws, knuckling over, very loose shoulders.

Secondary Faults A weak, long-legged, or dragging figure; body hanging between the shoulders; sluggish, clumsy, or waddling gait; toes turned inwards or too obliquely outwards; splayed paws, sunken back, roach (or carp) back; croup higher than withers; short-ribbed or too weak chest; excessively drawn-up flanks like those of a

Greyhound; narrow, poorly-muscled hindquarters; weak loins; bad angulation in front or hindquarters; cowhocks; bowed legs; wall eyes, except for dappled dogs; bad coat.

Minor Faults   Ears wrongly set, sticking out, narrow or folded; too marked a stop; too pointed or weak a jaw; pincer teeth; too wide or too short a head; goggle eyes, wall eyes in the case of dappled dogs, insufficiently dark eyes in the case of all other coat-colors; dewlaps; short neck; swan neck; too fine or too thin hair; absence of, or too profuse or too light tan markings in the case of two-colored dogs.

Approved January 12, 1971

Differences Between the Standards

It therefore becomes apparent that British and German Dachshunds are different today, whereas in the past, at the beginning of our love affair with the Teckel, the stock was founded completely on German imports.

I think it is important to point out that the present day German standard, originating as it does from the country of origin of the Teckel, has been adopted for the *whole* of continental Europe, as well as Central and South America.

We have already mentioned that the Germans have three sizes of Dachshunds, and that they are not actually weighed in the ring. The recommended size for the smaller Miniature is lighter than our British Dachshund, not more than 20lb (9kg), and that the classification is determined by a measurement around the chest (the maximum being 14in (35cm), and this measurement need only be taken *once* in a dog's lifetime, so long as it is after the age of fifteen months. The relevant judge issues a certificate, which will apply for the rest of that dog's life. This ruling should do away with any necessity to starve the dogs for future shows, which I think could be an advantage.

The German standard is more tolerant of a pincer bite, and although the scissor bite is the ideal, a pincer bite is not necessarily penalized as heavily as it would be in Britain.

The question of lowness to ground has always been a matter of differing opinions among some breeders. For some lowness to ground means that the dog can be almost touching the ground, although for most a realistic ground clearance, enabling the dog to do an active days work is more reasonable. Actually the German standard mentions that the ground clearance should be 'one third of the height from the withers', which is considerably higher than most British show dogs, but I understand that the German Teckelklub has now agreed to a clearance of one quarter, which would be more in keeping with the British standard.

3

The Pedigree

The Key to Success
by John Gallop

Scanning through the dog papers, or even reading books on the breeds, a newcomer today would scarcely be impressed by the importance of the pedigree in dog breeding. Of course books on genetics talk about them, but most people are apt, quite unfairly, to dismiss them as something to do with science and therefore mostly unintelligible! In any case, it is thought, people have bred animals for hundreds of years, and very successfully without any knowledge of Mendelism, so why shouldn't they go on doing so today? Well, the answer is they had their systems, and their systems were built on pedigrees.

The first thing a successful old-time breeder would have told you was that unless you were using some degree of in-breeding (I prefer to call it family breeding as many confuse the term with close in-breeding) you would not be breeding at all. In those days the general formula for establishing a line went something like this. Buy the best bitch you can afford and mate her to the best dog that matches her for type. With the first litter you have three possibilities: brother to sister, father to daughter or son to mother, the choice depending upon the quality and type of the individuals in the litter.

If you had sufficient resources, the advice might well have been to buy two bitches instead of one, preferably sisters and mate them to unrelated dogs. This way, you would have had the opportunity of mating cousins in the second generation.

While this advice still stands in principle, it is very much easier today, when there is a much wider choice of top-ranking stud dogs available. It would be foolhardy to say the least, to ignore the attainments and experience of the top kennels which make it so much easier to get to the point where you can establish your own strain. So how is the formula modified for today's conditions?

A precious handful! Joyce Gallop with her Champion Rhinefields Melanie, one of the early Rhinefields winners, Best of Breed at Crufts in 1957.

Well, the odds are that you bought your bitch from a well-known kennel (even if you did not it is probably closely related to one), so take it back and ask advice about which sire to use and do not be frightened of father to daughter matings. With the first litter, if you have to keep numbers down, you may keep only one or two bitches. Even if numbers are not a worry, it is unlikely that you will get more than two top-class bitches and you should only keep the best. The next generation should come from these bitches, again mated back either to the original stud or close relatives of him. The point is never to go outside the 'family' unless you have met with near-disaster and, if you have to, remember it will take at least two and probably more generations to get your type back. So the golden rule is to keep as close as you can to your original sire, always assuming he approaches your ideal.

Incidentally a little analysis of the pedigree of a well-known dog

Champion Rhinefields Cinderella Smooth, by Champion Rhinefields Corsair out of Rhinefields Catalina. Catalina was the top winning Smooth Dachshund bitch for 1967. Cinderella was bred from a brother and sister mating.

or bitch will reveal much of their breeder's technique and mode of thinking. One old breeding system illustrates this point rather well. It supposed that the influential lines were what was called tail-male to tail-female. This means that a litter was more the product of a sire's father mated to the dam's mother than simply of sire to dam. Of course this is not really true, but it does illustrate a point. The bottom line of a pedigree is of course entirely composed of bitches and the top line of sires. In dog breeding it is usually the owner of the dam that selects the sire, so if the bottom line comes from one kennel it is possible to work out the breeding plan. It can be a fascinating exercise, particularly if you are able to see the dogs in the ring or if not, in photographs. This is equally true on all lines of the pedigree and it is always worthwhile to follow a particular prefix through especially when the dog, or more probably the bitch, is not a champion. A glance at the Stud Book will quickly tell you whether its brothers or sisters were.

Most people would, I suppose, call this line-breeding. I prefer the term family-breeding and like to reserve line-breeding for the continual use of a particular dog or bitch's progeny mated to

The first three Rhinefields champions. Champion Rhinefields Melanie,
Champion Rhinefields Lenz, and Champion Rhinefield Falka.

distantly related animals. But you may ask why all this close breeding? The answer lies in the simple formula that like tends to breed like. Of course this means that the animals must look alike, but animals that look alike may have very different genetic make-up. The way to ensure that both their looks and genetic make-up are similar is to keep mating within the same family. Of course you may lose virility and people will tell you this is because of close in-breeding. But remember that loss of virility is in the same category as any other fault, can occur with pure out crosses and all faults have to be bred out.

Notice the expression 'bred out' – not 'bred away from'. If you are continually breeding away from faults, you will lose those positive good points you are striving to attain.

To show the success of in-breeding I often quote the case of the imported Smooth Dachshund, Champion Zeus vom Schwarenberg. One dog Champion Ingo von Luitpoldsheim occupied 15/32 of his pedigree (i.e. occurring 15 times out of a possible 32) and along with two sisters 27/32. Zeus became the ancestor of practically all the winning Smooth dachshunds in the fifties and sixties and many kennels inbred to him quite extensively.

A case like Zeus also highlights the importance of making sure that your pedigrees go back sufficiently far. Mostly you will find

79

three generations are quoted, but it has been my experience that one needs at least five. The reason is fairly simple. Few of us have sufficiently large kennels to be always using stock carrying our own prefix. There inevitably comes a time when one has to outcross, albeit within the family. Maybe one of your studs had mated a bitch who goes back to your line a couple of generations back. Their progeny will not then show up the family relationship on a three-generation pedigree.

Recently there have been several advertisements in the dog papers showing five-generation pedigrees of winning dogs, without a single name occuring more than once. One can only assume one of two things; either the breeder knew all the dogs by sight as well as reputation, or that there were one or two heavily inbred lines supporting the pedigree. It is uncharitable to assume they were only showing a pedigree as long as your arm! But I suspect they were really showing how many well-known animals appeared in these pedigrees. That is not the way to breed, but I suppose some people only expect to succeed by luck. Luck you need, but with ninety per cent of breeding, that winning strain is just one hard slog. You can take the quality of your dogs up to a certain point above the level of the common rut, but you need luck to produce that wonder dog. Without the pedigree, showing is like watching a football match – you have no influence on the result. With it the world can be your oyster and your peers will call it good breeding.

4

Selecting Your Dachshund

The Dachshund is unique amongst most dogs insomuch as there are six varieties and three different coats to choose from, which all come in two sizes in Britain, and three sizes on the continent. I think it is safe to say that all the varieties share those characteristics which we either love or hate. The Dachshund is bold, highly intelligent (especially when it is to his own advantage) and extremely loyal and affectionate. He is also *very* obstinate and self-willed. He makes the most wonderful companion, and will enter into the spirit of everything you do – the latter characteristic can be very irritating. If one is busy in the garden an inquisitive nose is *not* the best companion, and the same can be said for almost any task you undertake. I like the sketch I came across in an old German book of the busy gardener, planting out his young cabbage plants, whilst unbeknown to him his devoted Teckel is busy behind him, pulling them out! Alas, it has happened to me – my dogs love cabbages!

Of the three coats the smooth-haired is certainly the easiest to care for, he should only be bathed occasionally, and regular brushing and grooming with a chamois leather cloth will keep his coat in lovely condition. The long-haired dog will need more attention, and his feathering can become grubby, and he will need more brushing and combing, as well as trimming of the long hair on his feet. If you are fortunate enough to acquire a wire-haired with a good, harsh, correct coat, he too will not need a great deal of grooming, just a thinning out of the coat here and there, and trimming of the hair on the feet, which is best demonstrated to you by an expert. Should you have the misfortune to acquire a fluffy, soft-coated Wire, for which so many people fall for when they see them as puppies (they certainly are attractive), you will have a great deal of trouble in the future to keep the coat in show condition, if indeed you do decide to show.

If you are looking for a puppy because you have just lost a beloved Dachshund, you will probably be determined to replace

81

him or her with another one, exactly the same. This is certainly a mistake, for there were never two Dachshunds exactly the same; they are just as individual as people, and you will have to get to know, and to love your new companion, and to respect his different ways, all over again.

Take great care in the important selection of a puppy. It could be unwise just to answer any advertisement you chance upon in a journal. I well remember from my days in South Africa, that the South African Kennel Gazette had a quotation on the front cover (it

Keidon Kassandra and Champion Murantia Janine Marictur as a puppy.

possibly still does today), saying, if I remember correctly; 'He who invests in a puppy receives in return for that investment, ten years of love and devotion that he cannot purchase elsewhere at any price.'

My advice would be for you to contact one or other of the Dachshund breed clubs, perhaps the one nearest to you (a list of them appears in the Appendix). The secretaries of these clubs are dedicated Dachshund lovers, and will be glad to help you, if they can. Your local all-breed dog club might also be able to put you in touch with a local breeder, as could your vet, and even if this particular breeder does not have a litter at the moment, possibly he or she will know of someone who does, and the owner of a well-known stud dog is very often able to tell you where there is, or will be, a litter by their dog.

If you have ambitions to enter the show game, or to breed seriously, then you should certainly take very great care in selecting your early stock. You are unlikely to buy a great show winner as a puppy, although it *has* recently happened; if show winners were so easily bred, the dog game would loose a great deal of its excitement. Most of the serious breeders hope to keep the best puppy for themselves, as so often it is for that express purpose that they have bred the litter.

The 'best' puppy will not necessarily be the nicest character, for alas, the jolliest pup in a litter is so often *not* the glamorous show pup, so if you are just after a good companion, take heart, and if you are able to see the litter at an early age, you will be able to make your choice. It is best to see the litter from about five weeks upwards, as younger than that it would be difficult to pick out any particular puppy. Obviously you will have to come back later, when the litter is seven or eight weeks old, whenever the breeder allows the puppies to go to their new homes.

Things to Look For

Try to select a puppy with a good shining coat, cool nose and bright eyes. The pup who comes towards you wagging his tail could be a safe choice, he probably possesses a super temperament, but the cautious one who hangs back and sizes you up could turn into a lovely, intelligent chap; he is going to make sure all is well before rushing in.

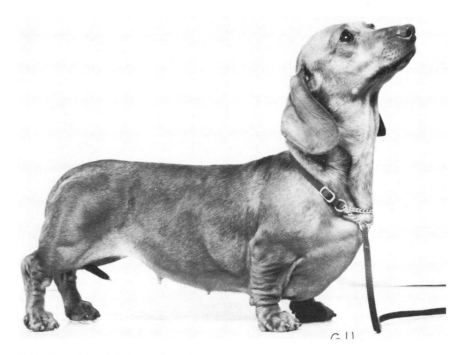

Safria Hannah – a Miniature Smooth.

You may have strong ideas as to which sex you want to own. Personally, were I choosing a puppy for companionship only, and had no ambitions to breed, I would select a dog. You will be spared all the fuss of your pet coming into season, and having to be isolated every six months or so. Yet there are those who maintain that bitches make superior companions to dogs, so it is up to you.

Nowadays there are both pills and injections which can be given to prevent a bitch coming into season, and your veterinary surgeon will be able to advise you about these. However, you *must* let a bitch have her first season normally, whatever you decide to do later, as to prevent this first oestrum could impair her development. Spaying (removing the ovaries) is another solution, which again is best left until the bitch is older, and fully developed.

When selecting your puppy try, if possible, to see that the pup has a correct scissor bite. At this tender age he will only have his deciduous teeth, but usually, if the bite is correct then, when the permanent teeth come through, they generally follow the same

A handful of mischief!

pattern. An undershot mouth seldom, if ever, rights itself, but an overshot mouth, if not too serious can do so. Later on, when the pup starts to teethe, he may go through several stages when the teeth look all wrong, but having been right to begin with, I usually find that they end up correctly. It is important later on when the permanent teeth are erupting, at between three-and-a-half months to about four-and-a-half months, to check on the canine teeth. Very often the deciduous or milk canines are retained whilst the permanent ones have erupted and this of course, might cause the teeth to go out of alignment, and spoil the bite. If they are loose, you can often help them by moving them, but if they remain firmly fixed you might have to have them extracted. These details do not matter unless you intend to breed or show. An incorrect bite would be heavily penalized in the show-ring, and a dog or a bitch with an imperfect mouth should never be bred from.

Sometimes a breeder will sell a puppy at a reduced price if the mouth is wrong, or indeed if there is any other visible defect which would impair the show potentiality of the pup, and if you just wish for a friend and companion, this could be the one for you.

Check that there are no dew claws on the hind legs; these do sometimes occur and the breeder should have removed them at about three days of age. Dew claws on the front feet are usually left on Dachshunds.

If you are selecting a male pup, try to ascertain that both testicles have descended into the scrotum. This might be difficult to see at an early age, but I usually find that at about eight weeks of age, when normally I let puppies go to their new homes, it is possible to see that both are present. Of course they can come down later, sometimes indeed several months later, but if you are aiming to breed or to show, it is important to know that the dog is 'entire'. Monorchids, dogs which only have one testicle descended into the scrotum, are capable of siring puppies, whilst cryptorchids, dogs which have no testicles present in the scrotum, are invariably infertile. Either of these conditions would be penalized at a show, and there is the risk that the undescended testicle might have to be surgically removed at a later date, as complications can occur.

As we have seen, except in chocolates and dapples, dark eyes, noses and nails are called for. A red Dachshund with lovely dark eyes is a delightful sight, and on the other hand pale eyes can look unattractive, especially in black-and-tans.

Watch the puppy running about. At this tender age he will look 'all over the place', but you can usually see if he is sound and strong on his legs. When buying your puppy, unless you are fairly knowledgeable, you are at the mercy of the breeder, and that is why it is so important to go to a reputable one, perhaps one who shows, and is the owner of well-known stock. If you have a knowledgeable friend, take him along when you make your choice. There is a saying in France, 'to lie like a dentist, and to be as dishonest as a dog breeder'; as my husband was a dentist, we had a lot to live down!

When you collect your puppy make sure that the breeder gives you a diet sheet, and he or she may offer you a temporary insurance cover, and, highly important, as well as a full pedigree, the breeder *must* give you a Registration Certificate from the Kennel Club together with a transfer of ownership signature. It is possible that you might have to wait for the Registration Certificate through no fault of the breeder, as the Kennel Club sometimes is slow in

Attractive pair of Miniature Long-hairs. Beau Geste of Woodheath and Tuonela Beachcomber of Woodheath.

sending them out. This document however, is most important, as without it you will be unable to breed, or to show.

The actual age at which you collect your puppy from the breeder may be as much up to him or her as to you; when I sell puppies I like them to go at an early age (from seven weeks onwards) if possible if the new owner is responsible and capable of giving that first special care and attention to a young puppy. I believe that at this age the change over to new owners and a new environment will be less traumatic than at a later date, and he will very quickly at this age recognize you as the new pack leader. However, I have breeder friends who do not like their pups to go to the new owners until they are over three months old, so you will have to come to an arrangement with the breeder. If you are just wanting a pet, you might like an older dog, one who is already trained and over puppy problems. They are not very easy to come by, as fortunately for Dachshunds, we have a very efficient rescue service, run by the Dachshund Clubs, and if any owner suddenly dies or for some reason has to find a home for his pet, there is usually a waiting list.

When you collect your pup, at whatever age, do ask the breeder about worming. Usually this will have been thoroughly done before the pup is collected, and later on, when you take your pup to the vet for his first inoculation (which is done at about twelve weeks of age), you can discuss further worming treatment with him.

5

Puppy Management

Clutching your pedigree, certificates, diet sheet and perhaps a supply of food to start you off with, you happily take your puppy home. Do not worry if he is car sick on the journey, they almost always grow out of it, but a thoughtful breeder will not have fed him too soon before your leaving, so you will be able to comfort him with a nice meal as soon as you get him home.

At first it is wise to follow the diet that he has been used to, but if you wish to change it, do so very gradually, in order not to upset him. Young puppies very often pass loose bowel movements, and unless they are *very* watery or smelly, and continue over a long period, this condition is not serious. It is often due to overfeeding, and the fact that the diet at this early age is very liquid.

When I sell a puppy I give the new owner the following leaflet:

Guide to Feeding

At seven to eight weeks of age:

7 a.m.   (or thereabouts). Baby cereal, wheat flakes or brown bread soaked in warm milk – about a small saucerful.

10.30 a.m.   2oz. (about $1\frac{1}{2}$ dessertspoonfuls) minced raw or cooked meat (or cooked chicken, scrambled egg, tinned puppy food or flaked cooked fish), to which add about $1\frac{1}{2}$ tablespoons of previously soaked puppy meal (the meal may be soaked with warm milk, meat stock or chicken juice). Do use a good quality meal.

2 p.m.   Warm milk with cereal, etc. as at 7 a.m.

5–6 p.m.   Meat meal again, as at 10.30 a.m.

Last Thing   Milk feed, as at 7 a.m.

'I am going to grow into a beautiful lady.' Tessa Thomas' young Miniature Long-haired puppy.

'What a lovely thing to catch and kill!' Champion Marictur Black Modiste, aged six weeks.

Add a few drops of cod liver oil, or a similar pet oil, and a calcium supplement, to one meal per day, amounts will be indicated on the tin. These are available from good pet shops.

As the puppy grows, increase the size of the meals. At about three months of age the meat can be chopped, instead of minced, and the 2 p.m. milk feed can be discontinued. At about four months old you should use about 3oz of meat per meat meal. At about six months of age give three meals per day, and the amount of biscuit meal, which by now will be the adult type, should have increased.

By twelve months old the dog will be on an adult diet. My own dogs usually get two meals per day, in the early morning and the late afternoon. They are meat and biscuit meals containing about 3oz of meat per meal. Cooked vegetables, such as carrots or greens are very good added to the meals, and it is a good idea to soak the biscuit meal in cabbage water, when available. When my dogs have finished their meal, they have a treat of a few raw leaves of cabbage or stalk ends, usually taken from the hard white cabbages. They love them, and really look forward to that moment.

Remember with your new puppy that rest is almost as important as food to begin with. When the puppy shows signs of tiredness, put him away in a quiet, warm place to sleep. He will let you know when he wants to wake up and play again! Do not let him get cold or wet. Contact your veterinary surgeon about inoculations, which are usually done at about twelve weeks of age. Until these are done, the puppy must be kept away from strange dogs and public places.

Early Training

This feeding guide is of course intended for Standard Dachshunds, Miniatures will require less, and it is indeed difficult to lay down hard and fast rules, as all dogs can vary as to their requirements, some being more active and using up more energy than others, and thus requiring more nourishment. Some puppies can go through a most irritating fussy stage. I have recently had one who turned his nose up at the most attractive things that I tried to tempt him with, and I thought I would never win the battle; then suddenly, for no reason at all that I could discover, he started to enjoy his food, in fact to wolf it all up, whatever it was, so under these circumstances, patience is all that is required. This is however, very rare indeed, for Dachshunds are a very greedy breed, and it is usually a question of keeping food from them, rather than tempting them to eat.

Training your puppy will need patience. If the breeder has trained the pup to 'go' on newspaper, this is a great help, as you can then put paper down near his bed or sleeping quarters (usually the kitchen), and hopefully he will oblige by using it. When he has had a meal, or when he wakes up from a sleep, pop him out into the garden, as these are usually the times when he will oblige by spending a penny, or more. Habit is a great thing, and gradually he will know that the garden is the right place.

A Dachshund need *never* be smacked. A verbal rebuke is usually quite enough, as he is a sensitive and intelligent dog, and will only want to please. For real naughtiness, a rolled up newspaper, banged on furniture or the floor (never on the dog), has a terrific effect.

Keep to the same timetable if possible, and use the same expressions, or words of command. You will find that he will quickly recognize quite a few sentences, especially if they are to his advantage.

You will not be able to take your puppy out from your own garden until he has had his course of injections against distemper and parvovirus, etc. so his initial lead training will have to be done at home. Firstly get him used to wearing a collar by putting it on for short periods. At first he will scratch and try to get it off but when he tolerates it the next stage will be introducing the lead. At first he will buck around and try everything he knows to get free, so great patience will be required to accustom him to it, and being led by it. Make it a great game at first, and a happy, laughable occasion, so that he will soon associate it with pleasure. Once you can take him out into the wide world there will be no problem, he will then certainly associate his lead with the excitement of a walk.

Nowadays we are spoiled for choice in the matter of collars and leads – as well as the old leather ones there are choke chains and mesh collars. I favour a type of choke chain, which tightens round the throat if the dog pulls too much. I consider this a safeguard; in a state of panic, if the dog were to become alarmed at something he could slip an ordinary collar, and perhaps become lost or run over. These accidents *do* happen, even with the best behaved dog.

Find out if there is an obedience training class near you. When your puppy is about six months old it is a very good idea to take him along. Not only will he learn some useful words of command, but he will become socialized with all the different types and breeds of dog that he will meet at the class – he will enjoy it thoroughly, and I am sure that you will too. As well as obedience classes most dog clubs run 'Ring Training Classes'. Do not be put off by this rather grand sounding name if you have no show ambitions for your dog. If you *do* have show ambitions, they will be essential, but even for training your young pup to mix with other dogs and people on a social level, they are most useful.

Your new puppy will probably sleep in the kitchen, so select a suitable, draught-free corner and give him his own bed or box there. Wicker baskets are completely unsuitable for Dachshunds as they are great chewers, especially during their teething period, which is up to about six months of age, and some of them will chew *everything* in sight! In my early days, in a state of blissful ignorance, I gave my new puppy a lovely smart wicker basket, and within a few months it was reduced to a basket bottom, with a few miserable spikes sticking up; very dangerous as well as useless. Foam-filled duvet-type dog beds are very popular today. Dachshunds love them – they are warm and so comfortable – but never, until your friend is too old to care, leave him alone with it at night, or when you go out. I have done so and on my return was greeted by a sea of plastic foam all over the kitchen, and a torn duvet, plus some very guilty looking Dachshunds. However, I stuffed the foam back, sewed up the cover, and nowadays it serves as a special bed for them on sunny days in the garden, but never to be left alone with!

'We are waiting and ready for our walk.'

There are very good heavy plastic beds available nowadays in all sizes at good pet shops. These are ideal, and they will last for ages. Dachshunds of course, being Dachshunds, will still chew at the edges, but they can do little harm either to the bed or to themselves, and it could even help their teething problems. These beds can be scrubbed down every so often with disinfectant. I usually put newspaper in the bottom and a half blanket on top, and this makes a very cosy bed. The type of bed on an iron frame, slightly above the ground is also good, slightly more expensive, but very nice as it raises the dogs above any ground draughts. If you have more than one dog I think each should have his own bed. They will undoubtedly all end up in the same one, usually piled on top of each other, but nevertheless they should have the choice.

One Dachshund alone is very unlikely to take to sleeping outside in sheds or kennels, but if you intend to take up breeding, and are acquiring several dogs, then obviously this could be your wisest plan. Invest in a good type wooden kennel; there are many types and sizes, and you will be able to see them on display at all the bigger dog shows. In the cold weather it will be essential to run some sort of heat to an outside kennel. One of the infra-red lamps suspended over the beds at a safe height is the ideal method. You can enclose the kennel in a run of chain-link fencing, as large as you have space for, but do remember to sink the wire in a trench, because the Dachshund has been bred to dig, and he could dig his way out. Around the house itself it is a good idea to have paving stones, or a concrete area, making a suitable place for the dogs to sit outside in the sun. Use grass or clinker for the rest of the enclosure. If the run is large enough you can make a small, low platform – the dogs will enjoy jumping up and down from this, or lying underneath on a really hot day. A friend of mine has fitted old drain-pipes (the big ones) in her dog runs, and the puppies have terrific games with them, hunting each other up and down the tunnel, and displaying all their inborn expertise for the hunt.

Bedding in the outside kennels could be the usual plastic beds with paper and blankets, which must be scrupulously washed and changed, or use wood wool, which can be so easily changed and disposed of when it becomes soiled. Wood wool is available in bales, and if you can locate a suitable supplier they will deliver. I certainly do *not* advocate the use of straw as bedding material. It is certainly cheaper, and much easier to come by, but you could be letting yourself in for a lot of trouble if you use it. Most will obviously have come from farms, and however wonderful the farm, mice and other creatures will have been around in it, and in consequence you could introduce skin troubles or other pests with this bedding.

The house dog as well as the kennel dog must always have fresh water to hand – use a suitable non-tip water bowl in which the water is changed each day. Puppies tend to tip over the bowls, so make sure that they are of the type that they cannot get a grip on. Nowadays there is a great variety and choice of feeding bowls. I think stainless steel ones are ideal, as you can safely boil them but enamel ones are also very good, although they do tend to become chipped, and could harbour germs. Plastic bowls are not so good, they are the least hygenic, and it is very important, especially with the puppy, to maintain scrupulous cleanliness. Please, *never* let him feed off your own dishes – get him several of his own, and stick to them. He will be much happier. Always feed at the same time, if it is possible, the puppy as well as the adult dog soon gets into a routine, and this gives him a sense of security.

Give the puppy lots of safe things to chew and to play with. Rubber toys are fine, but do be certain that they are strong, solid

Champions all in a row! Four little Drakesleat Miniature Wires, all champions, look up to their kennel companion, the Irish Wolfhound – also a Drakesleat champion.

rubber and therefore are not easy to destroy and to swallow. The same ruling applies to balls, which all puppies and indeed most adult dogs love all their life – make sure that they are solid and cannot be easily chewed up, but also not so small that they could swallow them. This is very important, has often happened, and a big vet's bill for removal has been incurred! Shin bones make good toys, and they are wonderful for the teeth, but it is highly important that they are solid, and will not splinter, so a careful watch must be kept whilst the pup or dog enjoys them. Here a useful training session could be for you to make sure that the puppy will let you take the bone away from him without growling at you – one of the little opportunities to demonstrate that *you* are top dog and master in your house. An old dish cloth or thick rag, with a knot tied in the middle, makes a really grand toy. My dogs love them – they have terrific tugs of war, and they proudly 'kill' them, but they must then be trained to bring them to you, and let you take them.

Your pup will have his first inoculation, usually done in two parts, at about three months of age, and thereafter once a year. This routine inoculation protects against distemper, hepatitis, leptospirosis and parvovirus, so is indeed a must for all dogs. Normally no reaction is noticed from the injections. Regular worming, with pills supplied by your vet is recommended once very six months or so. Once your pup is safely inoculated he may start going for regular walks and exercise, but do not over exercise him at first, and remember that he will still be growing until he is about twelve months old. Once he is fully grown a Dachshund can do with any amount of exercise; he has been bred as an active, vigorous dog, fit to hunt and dig and trail, *not* as a lap dog.

6

Adolescent and Adult Care

The Dachshund is normally a healthy, active dog, and given suitable quarters, sensible feeding and regular exercise, combined with lots of love and attention, he will reward you by returning your love in full measure, and will be your loyal companion and guard for his entire life.

He is certainly one of the easiest breeds to groom, and the Smooth especially needs very little attention. Make sure that his booster inoculations are always up to date, and that his bedding, basket and food bowls are cleaned and disinfected.

Champion Yatesbury Evening Star. 'Dick' was one of three brothers, all of whom were to become champions. His two brothers are Champion Yatesbury Big Bang and Champion Yatesbury Evening Echo.

Weekly Care

It is a good idea to make a habit of having a weekly 'do over' to check ears, nails, eyes and so forth, and make sure that his teeth and coat are clean. Dachshund ears need to be inspected because their pendulous shape means they are slightly more prone to canker than some other breeds. Clean them out with cotton wool and antiseptic and if they seem to harbour a lot of dirt (which could breed mites) get some drops or powder from your vet. Nails, too, should be clipped about once a week, and some dogs seem to need this attention more than others. If you exercise your dog regularly on hard surfaces, such as roads, this can help to a certain extent to keep the nails short. If you have paved paths in your garden this also will help to keep feet trim, and the legs strong.

A dog can be 'down on his pasterns' through too much running about all the time on soft ground. You will have to acquire proper dog nail clippers from a good pet shop (I like the guillotine type), and you will have to accustom your dog to undergo this operation from a very early age. He will doubtless try to resist it, so do be careful not to cut too much off at first, because should he get really hurt, which of course is what he fears, then it will be even more difficult the next time. It is best to have help during this operation. Ask a friend to hold him really firmly, and then you must insist on carrying out the job – perhaps by several stages, but you must assert your authority in a strong but kind manner.

Regular inspection and cleaning of teeth is recommended. Dogs fed on soft food can get a build-up of tartar, which can cause problems in later life. Get your dog accustomed to having his teeth scrubbed from an early age. You can use a special dog toothpaste, or salt water, or the powder-type toothpaste (especially formulated for smokers) can be most effective. Apply it via dampened cotton wool. Give hard biscuits to chew, and safe non-splintering shin bones.

Care of the Coat

Regular brushing with a good firm bristle brush will keep the coat in shining condition. For that extra gloss (useful at a show), a rub over with a chamois leather or a velvet hound glove works wonders. This regular brushing will help to keep at bay those loose hairs which

Champion Berrycourt Scarlet, by Champion Berrycourt Blackthorn
out of Berrycourt Sweet Charity.

end up all over the house and on clothes. Dogs should be kept off the chairs and furniture, although sometimes this is a struggle. A very firm voice is needed. I like the cartoon I once saw of a sofa, piled high with Dachshunds of every size and type, and the poor unfortunate owner crouched up in a corner!

Long-haired and wire-haired Dachshunds do of course need slightly more attention to their coats than do the Smooths. If you are blessed with a harsh-coated Wire, he will not require much trimming. He and his long-haired brother need a little trimming on the feet, and check that the whiskers around the mouth and the backside are kept clean, as they can become dirty in long-coated dogs. You can get a special trimming knife at good pet stores which helps to keep the hair of the Wire in order, but if your Wire is of the kind who needs a lot of coat attention, your best plan is to go along to a knowledgeable breeder, and to get him or her to show you how to tackle the coat. Longs need their coats regularly brushed and combed out, to prevent knotting and to keep that glorious sheen, which is such a beautiful feature of this lovely variety.

Bathing too often can get rid of the natural oils in the coat, but of course you will have to give him the occasional bath, especially if he has obliged you by rolling in something foul (delight to him), on his walk. Use a good dog shampoo. Have the water just nicely warm (use a tub, the sink or the bath) and stand the dog in it and then thoroughly soap him all over, according to the directions. Make sure that you rinse him really well, and have lots of towels handy to envelope him when you lift him out. Do dry him as much as possible before you let him go, because his first action will be to shake himself vigorously, and you could get thoroughly soaked in the process. Rub him well down again, and make sure that he does not get cold afterwards. A biscuit treat after any of these grooming ordeals is a good plan, Dachshunds being so fond of their grub that they might even think it all worthwhile!

Feeding

A fully grown Dachshund needs two meals a day; a small one in the morning, and a main meal in the late afternoon. Adjust these times

International Champion Cratloe Double Topping, by Champion Andyc Topper out of Cratloe Dream Topping. Double Topping won eleven CCs and was the sire of nine champions.

A trio of well marked chocolate dapples. Chocolate Truffle of Burrowsdine and her daughters Deepfurrows Silver Charm and Deepfurrows Silver Sixpence.

to suit your own convenience, but do endeavour to keep to the chosen times, as the dog is a creature of habit, and he will very quickly learn when his meal is due. Regular times and habits will give him a sense of security. I give about 4oz meat (tinned or cooked pet mince meat) plus a good biscuit meal (previously soaked), for the main meal, and a similar one, but with less meat, for the smaller meal.

You can very successfully feed your Dachshund on any of the reputable 'Complete Feeds', and in that case follow their instructions. With these complete feeds no additives should be necessary. Personally I like to use a non-complete biscuit meal, and therefore I give meat, and add mineral supplements, in the form of powders or tablets. Calcium (for growing youngsters and in-whelp and feeding mothers), cod liver oil and wheat germ oil (especially good for breeding stock) should also be given when indicated. Directions as to amounts are always given on the packages. Many people swear by garlic as a blood purifier, and it is believed to keep worms at bay. Most reputable herbalists stock quantities of these medicines especially formulated for dogs, and they usually have stalls at dog shows or country events.

It is quite normal for dogs to occasionally eat grass, and they will usually be sick afterwards. Do not worry, it is just nature's way of cleaning out the system. I find that dogs vary in their liking or otherwise of vegetables. I personally do *not* agree with a complete vegetarian diet for the dog. Nature intended him to be a carnivore. You can, with great benefit, accustom him to like some vegetables. I give carrots and cabbage, either raw or cooked, and they look upon cabbage, especially, as a real treat. The leaves from the hard, white cabbages are the ones they love.

General Well-Being

You can usually tell when your pet is off colour. Apart from a change in behaviour pattern, take note if there is a lack of interest in food or the daily walk. Other signs could be dullness of coat or eye, dry nose, running eyes, loose bowel movements (blood in them a very definite warning sign) etc. When in doubt it is advisable to take his temperature. Use a blunt-ended thermometer, inserted for about one minute in the rectum, to take the temperature. The normal dog temperature is 101.5°F (38.6°C) and certainly if in any doubt obtain veterinary advice.

Never let your Dachshund run up and down stairs – the strain of so doing, and the jolting on the spine could cause trouble. Many of my friends have fitted child-proof type gates at the foot of their stairs to prevent this. The Dachshund is a great jumper; being low to ground he is constantly trying to jump up and greet you, and to show his love. Try to prevent too much of this, as not only do your smartly dressed visitors object, but it does put a strain on the back.

Dachshunds get on very well indeed with children if they grow up with them in the family, and likewise they will tolerate cats in their own family, if they have known them from puppyhood. I found that my dogs respected their 'own' cats, but would still delight in chasing other cats, if they got the chance!

It is certainly important to socialize your dog as much as possible, to get him accustomed to other dogs (especially other breeds), and to strange people. For this, training classes, either ring craft or obedience, run by your local dog club are the ideal way for him to meet other dogs, even if you do not intend to show him.

Most dogs love to go out in the car. Train him from the earliest age to sit quietly on the back seat. He will love to watch the passing world from the car windows, and when he is used to it, he will wait for a long time, happily watching for your return. You can of course

Amber of the Moat. Bred by Mrs Rice Evans.

invest in a dog guard for the car, and make him a cosy bed there. Should he be car sick as a pup, do not lose heart, as they nearly always grow out of it, and you will find that travel sickness pills, either veterinary or human, will help cure this. Make sure when you leave him in the car that there is a window open (obviously not so much that he could jump out), and *never ever* leave him in the car, even with windows open, if the weather becomes really hot. This has been the death of more dogs than one likes to think and it is simply owing to thoughtlessness on the owners' part.

Travel and Exercise

A crate is a very useful piece of equipment. You can get many types nowadays, some of which are very easily collapsable, and therefore easy to carry. You can use these in your car, or at home, or indeed if you do start a show career they will be a 'must' for convenience at open shows, where there is usually no benching. If you invest in a

Hand in plastic bag about to pick up faeces.

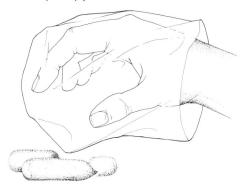

crate it is a good idea to use it around the house and to accustom your dog to go in it for longish periods, perhaps giving him a bone treat or such whilst he is inside. He will very soon get used to it, and indeed some dogs like them so much that they will go in of their own accord. Having trained him to like this little refuge you will always have a secure place to put him, should visitors arrive, or workmen, or some such contingency.

When you take your dog out for his walks, make sure that he is on a secure lead, and preferably a choke chain or chain collar. In emergencies ordinary collars can so easily be slipped, and the dog escape, whereas the choke chain will tighten around the neck. They very soon will become used to these chains, and it prevents the dog pulling too much on the lead, which can become exhausting, to both dog and human. Only let him loose if you have already trained him to come back to you on command (perhaps by the use of titbits), or if there is no traffic or farm animals about.

It is very important not to let your dog foul a public place or footpath. Many devices are sold in the way of scoops and the like, but one of the most effective ways to remove faeces is to carry a small plastic bag, reversing it over your hand to pick up the offending matter. You can then easily throw it into the rubbish bin.

The pleasure that your dog will get from short walks, even should they be through ugly streets, is immense. His sight is indeed excellent and very long, but he sees life in shades of grey, and beauty of scenery means nothing to him, although this lack is made up in full measure by that wonderful nose. As we have seen, in the early days our Teckel had the German Bloodhound in his ancestry, which accounts in large degree for that wonderful sense of smell. A

'The brave smell of a stone.'

walk will become an enchanted occasion of delightful perfumed experiences; I am sure that if we could chat to him he would be able to describe in detail every little creature that had passed along that path in the last couple of days. His nose possesses over two hundred million more smelling cells than does a human nose, and his brain cells are also more aligned to analyse those smells.

G.K. Chesterton, in his poem *Song of the Dog Quoodle*, starts Quoodle off by saying:

> They haven't got no noses,
>   The fallen sons of Eve;
> Even the smell of roses
>   Is not what they supposes;

and I particularly love the lines:

> The brilliant smell of water,
>   The brave smell of a stone.

Most Dachshunds will enjoy these daily walks right up to the end of their days. They may get a little slower, and more sedate, but a dignified stroll down the lanes is a must. Dachshunds usually live to a good age, and are active right up to the last – I suppose twelve years is around the average. They may have lost a little of that wonderful sense of smell, and sometimes their eyesight is not quite so good, but so long as they are still enjoying life, and still enjoying their daily food, all is well.

7

Training Your Dachshund

by Val Beynon

All dogs, Dachshunds included, are very little different from their wild ancestors. The thin veneer of civilization is all that covers the instincts and attributes of a wild animal. They were designed for a particular lifestyle, and because their normal behaviour made them of use to early man, they were an attractive prospect for domestication. Over many thousands of years, man has developed the dog into a diversity of breeds – sizes, shapes and colours, of amazing variety. At the same time, the natural behaviour of the dog has been modified – some instincts being allowed to lapse, and others encouraged. In spite of this, nearly all dogs have almost all the original set of behaviour patterns to some degree.

If we are to train our dogs in any way, it is useful to consider what they were originally intended to do. The key to the understanding of the dog's mind is the fact that, not only is he a hunting animal, but he is a pack member, unlike say, the cat or the fox. A puppy brought up with humans is quite prepared to be part of their pack – he looks at the family from a canine point of view, and no doubt sees things we might miss! He knows that life depends on co-operation, but he is also prepared for a struggle up through the ranks of the pack, until, maybe one day, he will be the pack leader. If he is not to be the leader himself, he does not sulk, or spend his days saying 'If only . . .', as a human might do but accepts his place with a good grace, and supports and admires his superior. So, it follows, that if we are to train a dog to do anything at all, then that dog must regard the trainer as his pack leader, otherwise the dog will be training the owner – and that is not at all unusual!

Now we will consider the working of a pack of hunting dogs, and try to recognize the behaviour when we see it in our own household pets. Firstly, the pack leader will decide when the hunt is to start and great excitement begins in the pack, such as we have all seen

106

This little dog was the first Dachshund to win an Obedience Class in Britain. He is Firs Kaptor and won at Crufts in 1939.

when we reach for the lead. Then the pack moves off, the leader running in the front. (Does your dog pull on the lead, or hang back?) They use both noses and eyes when the prey is seen, and the dogs lower down in the pack will run round it, in the typical 'herding' manner we see in collies when working with sheep. I did not think this behaviour existed in Dachshunds – I have never seen any of mine do this, but I was recently told about two Standard Smooths who could round up sheep to the manner born.

After the kill, the pack will try to carry off as much as they can, first by bolting food until they can hold no more (all Dachshund owners know they can do this) and then, perhaps carrying some home as well, for puppies and nursing bitches left at home. Retrieving starts here but as this is of very little use to a short-legged dog, the Dachshund has not been developed as a retriever and some have very little idea of picking up and carrying (ripping up, yes – carrying, no!). Some do, however, and probably, the long-haired variety are the most likely to try to retrieve, as there is still just a trace of spaniel left in them.

Reactions between pack members are interesting – mainly consisting of cringeing and crouching postures from the low-ranking dogs, with lying down, and even rolling over. Meanwhile, the high-ranking dog pays little attention, and may even growl to reinforce the social position. So, thinking about our own dogs, we may wonder, if one of them absolutely refuses to lie down on command, is it because he considers himself as good as us? And, does he respect us less because we make such a loving fuss of him? Of course, if the dog is very nervous and unsure, then our petting will help a lot – we are in fact saying 'you are wonderful – perhaps you are higher up the social scale than me!' On the other hand, it is also possible to help a nervous dog by saying (in dog language): 'I'm the pack leader – just do what I tell you and don't worry!'

The best dog of all, I think, is the 'Napoleon' among dogs – the natural pack leader. Strong and determined, probably very intelligent, he would be the ideal leader of a wild pack. In the right human hands, he is a dog to be proud of. In the wrong family, he is bad news! As Napoleon grows up, he begins to get ambitious, and starts his rise to the top by challenging the lowest members of his pack – the old dog, or the smallest child. He does not bite the baby out of jealousy so much as ambition ('Surely I rank higher than this pup?'). If he gets away with it, he will inevitably try the older children next, and then the wife – he may not even have to bite anyone to establish who is superior to whom. The next one along the line is Dad and this is often when I am asked for advice – 'He bites all the rest of the family, but I can control him with the broom'. I'm not making this up, I took that little bitch from the family, and she was one of the best I ever had. Yes, it was a bitch in that case, though Napoleon is usually male! I do realize that about fifty per cent of Dachshunds and their owners are female, but if many of the difficult dogs are male, many of the people trying to deal with them are female!

At this point, it is as well to remember that we are talking about Dachshunds – and all Dachshunds were developed with the idea that they should go out and hunt and kill. I have known Dachshunds who have killed cats, birds, chickens, budgies, guinea pigs, pet rabbits, bantams, kennel mates, snakes, hedgehogs and even badgers. It takes a good dog to do this – but nowadays we do not encourage wholesale slaughter. Nevertheless, these are not nasty, evil, wicked dogs – they are real Dachshunds, perhaps the best of their kind, and the failures have been with their owners, in training and management. The big, strong dominant dog is one to treasure, and if his handler can prove himself a stronger pack leader, then he will have a second-in-command worth having.

Obedience Training

By now you should realize that everything depends on what your character is like, and how it fits in with the character of the dog you wish to train. It will also depend on the physical and mental abilities of you and the dog, and the strength of his various instincts.

By far the best way to learn to train a dog, is to attend a dog training club. The only problem at the club will be that few instructors treat handlers of small dogs seriously. I myself ignored the elderly lady with the male Yorkshire Terrier called Mitzi ('I think it's such a pretty name!') until they began winning club competitions, and ended up as the stars of our demonstration team.

The basic exercises in the obedience tests in this country comprise 'heel work', on and off the lead, including right angle turns to left and right, and about-turn to the right. Then there are 'stay' exercises of varying lengths, in the three positions – sit, stand and down. The next exercise is the 'recall' where the dog is left by the handler, usually sitting, and then called to the handler. The last of the novice tests is the retrieve of a dumb-bell.

Above novice level, there are more interesting tests – scent discrimination, send-away, fast and slow heel work – but it is impossible to cover more than the very basic training here. If you join a club, and start entering obedience classes (perhaps at exemption shows) or in club competitions and matches and start to win the odd card, then you will be learning the rest for yourself.

It is important to train your puppy to stand on the table and be examined by the judge.

Equipment

Before you start, there is the equipment to consider. Nothing as expensive as, say, fishing, or golf equipment but there is a strange reluctance on the part of would-be dog trainers to actually go out and buy the right article! For you, it is soft shoes and no clothing that dangles, flaps, or swings anywhere near the dog's face. You might be surprised to see people try to train dogs in full length skirts, boots with bobbles hanging from them, scarves trailing on the ground, gum boots, stiletto heels, and more.

For the dog, it is even more important. A lead, fairly long, and thin, flexible leather is the best but anything at a pinch, except chain. You are going to use the lead in several ways and it must be comfortable to hold, and allow you to get at least a yard away from your dog. At the dog's end of the lead is a more important piece of equipment, a collar. This should be a slip chain collar, which is not part of the lead. (When you do any exercise which requires the dog to be off the lead, and you have to take off the collar as well, it often seems to give the dog the idea that he is no longer under control.)

I have seen people train dogs in jewelled poodle collars, studded bull terrier collars, halties, body harnesses, nylon slip collars, and many others. Most of them did teach their dog something but how much easier it would have been to use the right equipment. Do not fall into the error of thinking that small dogs do not need choke chains – size has little to do with it. When a dog is wearing a properly fitted chain collar, not only does the handler have complete control, but when the dog has become used to the collar, he can pick up the slightest movement of the hand by the sound of the chain by his ear, and thus the handler has the full range of communication, from a gentle reminder to strong compulsion. I should stress that this is dependent on the chain being just right for the dog.

Choke chains, or check chains, as many people prefer to call them, come in many sizes. For a Standard Dachshund, I like a chain about 16in (40cm) long, or shorter, if you can get it over the dog's head. This way, there is no more than a couple of inches spare when you pull it tight, and the chain does not hang in a big loop when you take the lead off. The actual chain should be of the close-linked type, in as heavy a gauge as you can get in the size – it is difficult to get the heavy links in the shorter lengths, but get the best you can. Three or four links to the inch will be about the usual size, and, if you can

Champion Landmark Magician standing for the judge.

obtain it, get one made in flattened links. These links slide over each other very easily, thus producing a momentary pressure followed by instant release, which is just what we want.

Unsuitable chains include the so-called 'watch chain' collars (show collars, really,) the ones with big round, lumpy chains that do not 'run' properly, and all forms of double chains and set chokes. I know a lot of people do use these, but I am thinking of people who are starting out to train for the first time, and I think you need all the help you can get in the initial stages. Once in a while there is a dog who is so 'neck sensitive' that he will fight the choke chain all the time, and if you are convinced that you have one of this type, then try something else but understand it will be harder.

The next step is to unite the dog and the collar! There are two ways the choke chain can be put on the dog and only one of these will produce the instant release. It is rather difficult to explain without a picture, but if you are in doubt, try the chain over your wrist, and you will see the difference. Briefly, when the dog is standing on your left, and the lead is attached to the collar, the link where the

111

chain goes through is just behind the dog's right ear. The piece of chain to which the lead is fastened should go on over the dog's neck, and not under its throat.

Lessons

Now, while you and the dog are standing there, we can have our first lesson. This is the HEEL position. Success is going to depend on both of you knowing what this is! If you are facing straight down the path, or towards the door, then the dog should be doing the same. Even more important, and difficult for a Dachshund – his whole body should be facing that way. His shoulders should be level with your ankle, and he should be quite close to you, certainly not more than 6in (15cm) away, and preferably less. If a Dachshund has a fear of being stepped on, and many have, then you have your first problem, and you must bring him as close as you can, and gain his confidence. Besides worrying about the dog's position, we may also have a quick look at ourselves – the handler should be standing up straight – do not adopt the crouching position beloved of trainers of small dogs! The lead is in the right hand, about waist level, with some slack. The left hand is ready to use, either for a little jerk on the lead if needed, or to touch the dog. The handler should also be looking at the dog, using the voice, with some titbits in a pocket for rewards. The small dry foods sold for cats seem to be very exciting to dogs, and are nice and clean to handle.

Now we will consider *Exercise 1*. This merely consists of you and the dog standing in the 'Heel' position, and teaching the dog to look at you. The command is 'Watch Me!', and you can use any means to make him do so – your hand, your voice, the lead, and the rewards. If he is looking at you, you will be praising him, and if he is not, you will be working to regain his attention. From time to time you can reward him with a titbit. It should be possible to build up gradually to be able to keep the dog looking at you for minutes at a time. This can be practised anywhere – in the house or in the garden.

Exercise 2 is walking forward with the dog walking at heel. There are five things to do: Get the dog's attention (Fido, Watch me!), use the dog's name (Fido!), give the command (Heel!), give a hand signal (pat your left leg with your left hand), and step off with your left leg. If the dog does not step off with you, give a jerk on the lead and then slacken it off again. Dragging the dog along never does

112

any good. The commands and signals can be anything you fancy – you can say 'Rhubarb' and pat your ankle if you like but do give some signal by body language, it means more to a dog than a human, as dogs normally communicate this way. When I say 'jerk' the lead, it is up to you to decide how much force to use. The fat, lazy Bullmastiff in my training club needs a different jerk to the slightly inattentive Miniature Dachshund. As you walk along, you will want to turn left or right, or even turn round and walk back the way you came. This is usually called a right about-turn, and as you turn to your right, and the dog has to run a little faster to remain at your side – you must not wait for him. In all these turns, try to tell your dog what you are doing ('Fido, Watch me, Fido, Heel!') and give little jerks on the lead. Some people even have a separate command for left and right, but do not worry too much about that to begin with.

Exercise 3 is sitting on command. All Dachshunds can sit, and the only problem is to teach them that when they hear the command, they do it. If you have the dog on the lead, and are doing a little heel work, when you stop, say 'Sit!' in a firm voice, and gently place your left hand on his rear end, and steer him into exactly the place you wish him to sit. Use that hand to praise him, and tell him you are pleased as if he had done it himself. When you have done this a number of times, he will probably begin to sit on his own – make sure he sits in the right place and do not praise unless he is there. If he is not, do not push him into place, but make him move himself – tap him gently to make him move, and praise him and reward him when he is there. Do not let him sit in a one-sided 'puppy sit'.

Exercises 2 and 3 are generally taught together and you can teach them in the garden, the garage or the hallway. It is useful to practise on the spot sometimes, taking single steps, turning left and right. All the time the dog is doing what you want, make sure he knows you are pleased. Do not do too much and do not allow the dog to become bored, confused, or otherwise unhappy. Make sure he gets a lot right, and reward him. Remember, you are trying to teach him that 'Heel' means an exact position – sitting or walking.

Exercise 4 is 'Stay'. Start to teach it in the 'Sit' position – on the lead, of course. The dog is sitting beside you, in the correct position. Hold the lead in your left hand above, and slightly behind his head. Give him the command 'Stay' in a rather hard voice, give him a hand signal with the right hand (I suggest a pointed finger, or show him the palm of your hand) then step away from him using the right foot first (another signal to tell him that this is not heel work) to the

113

Dogs in the stay position.

distance of about 6in (15cm). Stay there for about two seconds, do not allow him to move, return exactly to your first position, and praise him! He has just done a 'Stay'! Now it is just a question of doing it again and again, very slowly increasing the distance and time. At some point you will have to leave the lead lying down by the dog, and if you have a nice long lead, eventually you will be about 6ft (2m) away, for perhaps a minute.

Things to remember about 'Stays'. Never, ever use the dog's name when you are away from him unless you want to call him – if you think he looks as if he is going to get up, repeat 'Stay' or say 'No'. Basically, if he breaks a 'Stay', it is probably because you have progressed too fast. What you do if he does break the 'Stay', is critical. Do not go back saying such things as 'Oh, dear, you are a naughty boy!' because he may, with reason, assume you do not really mind. On the other hand, if you shout and wave your arms about, you may confuse and frighten him. I believe that many dogs, quite aware of what you want, still wish to get you back by standing up, or barking. You do not want that either, so on balance, I think that the best thing to do, is to go at once to the dog, say absolutely nothing, replace him firmly in the exact spot he has just left, then give him a very firm command, and leave him again – and this is the important bit – at a much smaller distance and for a much shorter time, and having made sure he does not get up, return and praise him enthusiastically.

Exercise 5 is the other position in which we ask the dog to stay, namely 'Down'. (I'm leaving out 'Stand' – when you have taught the other two, you can amuse yourself by working out a good way to teach it!)

The 'Down' position has a built in difficulty. It is a position of submission, and if the dog just happens to be one of the Napoleon type, he may strongly resent being placed in it. The standard method of teaching is to stand in the heel position, say to the dog, firmly and in a hard tone, 'Down', at the same time pressing on his shoulders, and if necessary, gently easing his fore paws forward. If he lies still happily, command 'Stay' and try to stand upright. When you can do this, then carry on as you did for the 'Sit'.

If the dog does not want to 'Down' on command, and makes this plain by growling, throwing himself about and so on, then I think the best way forward is to try bribery. If you can enlist the help of an assistant at food time, put the dog on a lead, let him see the assistant holding the plate a yard away, and lowering it to the floor. You must now force him to lie down for a few seconds before he gets it. Do not forget, lots of praise as well when he does – and time and common sense will get you a dog that goes down on command (at least, when he thinks there is something to eat!).

Exercise 6 'Recall'. In its final form, it goes like this: the dog is in the heel position. It is then commanded to stay and the handler walks a short distance away, turns round, and waits a few seconds. The handler then calls the dog, who comes smartly in and sits in front of the handler, and then, at the handler's command, the dog returns to the heel position. This last manoeuvre is called the 'Finish'. Now, we have already taught the dog to stay and to sit, so the vital piece of this exercise is the actual movement of dog to owner!

This is a difficult thing to teach even if you have absolutely no interest in obedience work! Most people try to teach their dog to come to them in circumstances that put the odds very much against success. It is no good calling the dog when he has just met a most interesting female friend or when he has just smelt a definite aroma of rabbits beneath the bush, or even when he calculates that the walk has been five minutes short. The time to teach it is when he is on a long lead, and he knows you have titbits in your pocket. When you are out walking, suddenly take three steps backwards, at the same time saying 'Fido, Come!'. Use a light, encouraging tone. Make sure, with the lead, that he comes quickly to you, in front, and reward him and praise him. Do it frequently – you are really trying to get an automatic reaction. At home, when you are sitting watching TV you can call him up when the advertisements begin. When he is doing it well, you can try it off the lead in the garden, but only if he is not occupied in any way.

When at last you are pretty sure of him, you can try it in the park, or in the fields. Meanwhile, you can start calling him, on the lead, from a sitting position, and gently pushing him into a 'Sit' in front of you. If you drag him in, and whack him into the 'Sit', you will undo all the good work you did in encouraging him to come to you in the first place! He is required to sit in front of you, in an absolutely straight line, and this is a little difficult to teach to a Dachshund. It will require a great deal of patience, bringing him in on the lead, giving him a supplementary command, 'Straight', telling him 'No' if he is crooked, tapping him gently into the correct position, and then praising him and rewarding him.

If you prefer, you can call your dog from the 'Down' position. There are times and dogs where this is a good idea and others, when it is not. I will leave you to think this out. I firmly believe that if you are to be a trainer, you must do an awful lot of thinking on the subject, putting yourself in the dog's place, working out how he becomes confused.

The final piece of the 'Recall' exercise is the 'Finish'. As this goes on the end of both the 'Recall' and the 'Retrieve', I shall treat it as exercise 7.

Exercise 7 The 'Finish' causes a lot of trouble. The first problem is caused by handlers always sending the dog to heel every time they do the 'Recall' or 'Retrieve'. If the reward is given when the dog is back to heel, you can imagine that the average Dachshund can see what is required, he thinks, and whips round to heel without a command, thereby losing the few marks that would have won your club the match! So, to avoid this, we generally teach the finish as a separate exercise, putting it on the end of the other two exercises only occasionally. Do it once in a while, or you will have a dog like mine, sitting grinning at me, refusing to go to heel, secure in the knowledge that I must be trying to trick him, as we never do 'Heel' after 'Come'.

The next complication is that there are two methods of getting the dog from in front of you back to heel. The usual one is to send him clockwise to your right and round behind you to your left side again. He will be out of your sight for a short while – I have known Dachshunds wander off in search of more interesting things, once behind their handler! On the other hand, literally, the alternative is for the dog to go to the left in a small anticlockwise circle, and end up once again, sitting straight at heel. This is not an easy movement for a Dachshund, perhaps easier for a Miniature than a Standard, but harder for a beginner to teach. So we will concentrate on the first method, and try to get the dog moving fast. Some trainers will say that a reward of food here will cause the dog to anticipate the command but with Dachshunds, I think a titbit is probably the best way to get the dog round quickly. How to teach this is best shown by diagrams but I will try to do it in words.

The dog is sitting nicely in front of you, get his attention, hold the lead in your right hand, and command 'Heel', at the same time stepping back one pace with your right foot only. If the dog does not follow the lead, jerk it and encourage him. When he is level with your right foot, change the lead behind your back to the left hand, and bring your right foot back beside the left one. Now change hands again, leaving your left hand free to make sure that when the dog re-appears on your left, he will sit, on command, in exactly the correct position. Now you can give him the reward, and make a great fuss of him.

Exercise 8 The 'Retrieve' is a hard exercise and will be the making of your partnership with your dog.

There are two basic methods of teaching a dog to retrieve, both of which have their place. The obvious one is play training – that is to say, you throw some article that he likes, and if he runs after it and picks it up, you encourage him to bring it back to you. This game can best be played by a puppy – if you are training an older dog, you may find the instinct to pick up toys has gone. If he will do this, keep on doing it but make sure you just regard it as fun – no commands, no recriminations, no bad feelings.

Parallel with this play, you should be teaching the dog to hold a specific article. Eventually you will want him to fetch a dumb-bell – essentially a short wooden bar with some sort of wooden ends that raise it from the ground, and make it easier for the dog to pick up. In

'Present'.

the initial stages, however, it is as well to start with something else, in case he takes a life-long dislike to a dumb-bell! I like to use a piece of short stick, well covered by something (the one glove you did not lose is perfect!). Tie it firmly with thin cord, and you should have an article about 6in (15cm) long and no more than 1in (2cm) thick, firm, and yet not really hard.

Now, you are going to harden your heart, and compel your dog to hold this in his mouth. By far the best place to do this is in the kitchen with the dog on the table. If your kitchen is too modern to have a suitable place, perhaps there is one in the garage. Put the dog's lead on, and lift him on to the table. Say 'Sit, Fido, Watch me!' Then gently open his mouth, and put the article in. In case of a struggle, open the mouth by putting your fingers in at the side. Be careful to place the article just behind the lower canine teeth and, because the dog's lips curl in over the teeth in the bottom jaw, be very careful indeed not to press down on the article. If he is struggling to spit it out, just put your fingers under his chin, and raise his head up. Only leave it in his mouth for a second or two to begin with, then take it from him. Do not let him drop it!

You will have noticed that I have not mentioned any commands and you must decide what you want to use. Many people use three – 'Fetch', 'Hold' and 'Give'. I have given this much thought, from the dog's viewpoint, and personally I say 'Fetch'. My dogs, who cannot speak English, imagine that 'Fetch' means 'Go and get that thing in your mouth and keep is there until I say 'Give''. So I start from the beginning saying only 'Fetch' and 'Give'. I should tell you that most trainers do not agree with me.

So here we are, patiently opening the dog's mouth, putting the article in as we say 'Fetch', waiting a very short while, saying 'Give', and taking it. The dog hates it, and to tell the truth, so do I. Of course, we are giving a reward each time we take the article, and praising him to the skies. At this point I usually move to some irresistible titbit – chocky drops, cheese or even boiled, cubed liver. Do enough – do not do too much and do not give up or lose your temper. I would suggest putting about a dozen of the treats on the window-sill, where the dog can see them, work through them, and then release him.

Sooner or later, I am not saying when, the day will come when the dog will suddenly realize that he has only to hold the article, and there is an endless supply of reward! When he opens his mouth himself, you know you are winning. When he reaches forward to take it, you are nearly there. When he lifts it from the floor, and holds it, you can cheer! Keep feeding the titbits, keep making it fun, and gradually encourage him to take a couple of steps to get it, do a little heel work carrying it, or do a recall, a short one, with it in his mouth. Then, maybe you can try throwing it a couple of feet away, and bringing him gently back, on the lead, to a 'Sit' in front. Now, as with all training, it is just a matter of developing what you have – giving the dog confidence, and making it all enjoyable to him. At some point you must change to a dumb-bell – do not leave it too long, or he may have decided that he only wants his original article. The material from the old article can, perhaps, be wrapped round the mouth piece of the dumb-bell, but be prepared to go back a few steps in training when you do this. If you are working at a club, then you may also find that the dog is several weeks further on in his training at home, than at the club. This is quite normal! Everyone's dog can always do it at home – so they tell me!

Entering Classes

When you can do all the exercises but the last, you can enter pre-beginners classes. When he can retrieve his old training article, you

A happy line of winners.

can enter beginners level, and when he can fetch the dumb-bell, he is of novice standard. Many exemption shows put on obedience classes – tests vary here and read through them carefully. Before you enter for the first time, you should watch other competitors at work, as there are various conventions that you need to know.

If you belong to a club, you will know how tests are conducted, but if you do not, you must compensate by, first working your dog where there are distractions, and secondly, you must at least watch other people working their dogs at a show.

Anyone coming into this absorbing hobby should go to the library and demand to borrow all the relevant books they have. Do not be surprised if the advice differs a lot from mine as there is an infinite number of ways to train a dog and I have tried to tell you the way that works best with my Dachshunds. There may be better ways to suit your own dog. Training a dog is not a precise science – it is more like tightrope walking, a difficult balance between compulsion and persuasion, always making decisions on when to praise and when to say nothing.

After some thought, I will summarize my advice as: be in control –

you must be the pack leader. Contrive that the dog does right, and then praise him. Teach him accurately and do not accept anything wrong. Make sure the whole thing is fun for you both!

I shall end by giving a special word of appreciation to my dear old imaginary dog, Fido, who has worked through many training classes with me, and has been helping me once again, to write this. You see, one thing you must never do is to use your real live dogs as demonstrations for training, to drag them about to show off, or anything other than one-to-one work, just you and your dog, trying to understand each other. Now, make a start – there are many things out there waiting to be discovered.

8

Making a Start in the Show-Ring

If you are aiming to start in the show world, and have had no previous experience, it would be wise to start taking one of the weekly dog papers; not only are they very interesting reading, but in them you will find notices of all the forthcoming dog shows, as well as the big Championship shows. There will be notices of smaller open shows, and even exemption shows, which can be entered on the day, and they are the ideal beginning for a novice, as well as being a great day out with your dog.

Go along, as a spectator to begin with, to some of the larger shows, and especially to the specialized breed shows; by attending these shows you will be able to get an idea of the procedure, and will be able to see good dogs in the show-ring, and see how they are handled, and what the judge requires of both dog and exhibitor.

Good handling of a dog in the ring is so important, and in the final decision by the judge it could just make the difference. An expert handler can make a mediocre dog look like a winner, whilst a poor handler can make a champion look nothing. Having said that, a good judge will be well aware of this, and he will get the dogs to move as much as possible, in order to judge each exhibit on its own merit.

If you decide that you want to have a go at showing, it is essential that you and your dog learn how to behave in the ring, and this you will be able to learn by going to the ringcraft classes, mentioned previously. They are run by nearly all dog clubs, and you will no doubt find that your local club runs classes. At the back of the book is a list of specialist Dachshund Clubs, and it would be a good plan to join your nearest one; all these clubs run their own shows during the year, several of them run Championship shows, and here you will be able to see Dachshunds going through their paces in the show-ring.

Champion Dianamo the Chief.

The brace class, for two animals as well matched as possible, is fun to enter. Here we see Pam Sydney's winning pair Champion Yatesbury Nanette and Yatesbury Kandida.

123

Champion Landmark Magician, aged seven months, winning the puppy stakes at the Three Counties championship show.

Hopefully, whilst you are attending these first dog shows, to get the 'feel' of things, you will find that some of the exhibitors will chat to you, and give you advice, but do remember that at the big shows everyone is busy, and anxious about their dogs, and their classes, so do not be downcast if they fail to give you much of their time.

You will not be able to show your puppy at any dog show held under Kennel Club rules until he is six months old, and all these shows have to be entered several weeks beforehand. In order to do this you will have to get a schedule from the secretary of the club, fill it in and post it off in good time. The classes which are scheduled vary slightly at different shows, but at most big shows and at the breed club shows, Dachshunds have separate classes for all their varieties. For instance, if you have acquired a Standard Smooth dog puppy, you will find a class, under the smooth-haired variety, for 'Puppy Dog', and then the usual classes are Junior, Novice, Post Graduate, Limit and Open. The schedules always give full definitions of these classes, and so you will be able to decide for which class your dog or bitch is eligible. It is pointless to enter a puppy or a young inexperienced animal in one of the senior classes, such as

Limit or Open, because these classes usually have the older and more experienced winning dogs in them. Some of the smaller shows have classes for Dachshunds which are scheduled as 'AV' classes – this means that all varieties of coat and size of Dachshunds will go into the same class and therefore in your 'AV Puppy Class' for instance you may find a Smooth, a Long-haired and a Wire-haired, and perhaps one of each size!

Exemption shows, notices of which appear not only in the dog papers, but usually also in the local press, mean that they are exempt from Kennel Club rules, and therefore they can usually be entered on the actual day of the show, and they will have lots of special classes, several fun ones, and if you are a complete novice these events are the ideal way for you to start a show career. You will see how your dog behaves when he gets into the ring, surrounded by others dogs, and you will get an idea of what is required by the judge.

The Dachshund needs little preparation for the show-ring, no special grooming should be required, he should always look in healthy shining condition. Naturally he should not be too fat, but that ruling would apply to the pet as well as the show dog, and he should need no special diet.

Malynsa Matchmaker, by Classridge Carbon Copy out of Classridge Cosiety.

Nowadays only the big Championship shows are benched. Here you will be given a number for your dog and you will find that you have a benching compartment reserved for him under this number in a special tent or area with all the other Dachshunds. You will have to take along a piece of blanket or similar bedding to put on the bench, and a show-chain (which you can purchase at dog shows or good pet shops) in order to secure him by the collar, to a ring which you will find in the bench. At first it may take a while for your dog to get used to being benched, so keep an eye on him and reassure him occasionally. You will be allowed to take him off his bench and either outside the tent at a country show, or into an exercise area at a big indoor show to relieve himself. Try to make sure that he has in fact done so before you take him into the ring to show him, as it can be a bit embarrassing if he squats down in the middle of the show-ring!

The time that actual judging will start is always indicated on the schedule, and normally these times are adhered to, so get to the show in good time, and then you will be able to relax and so will your dog.

The smaller shows do not have benching. It is always marked on a schedule as to whether there will be benching, so you will know beforehand. If the show is unbenched it is a very good plan to acquire one of the folding cages – you will find that most shows expect the exhibitors to come with these, and usually at a well run show there will be clearly defined areas where you will be permitted to put your show-cage.

When you actually take your dog into the ring try to behave with confidence, as a nervous exhibitor can transmit those nerves to his dog. Respect other dogs and other exhibitors in the ring, and keep your eye on the judge in order to see what is required. Also keep an eye on your dog to make sure that he is standing correctly, and is looking his best. Before you do enter a show you will almost certainly have attended ring training classes at your local club so you will be familiar with the method and your dog will be trained to stand on the table whilst the judge goes over him to assess his quality. A dog who fails to stand and show off his finest points on the table is at a great disadvantage, and indeed a dog who is a good 'show-off' could be half way to winning.

I often think that newcomers to the show game should not be blamed for sometimes being puzzled and confused by the final placings, and by the selection of winners. Obviously if all judges

A winning line of Ashdown Dachshunds.

thought exactly alike, and the same dogs always won, there would be little point in going to shows. It becomes apparent that the Dachshund Standard, as laid down by the Kennel Club, is open to different interpretation by different judges, and very often the clever exhibitor will discover what 'type' certain judges like, and will either follow him or avoid him. A judge has a great responsibility when performing his task, for his placings can influence the novice; having seen a particular dog gain high honours at an important show, they will be convinced that it must be the type to aim for.

Judging

If you have ambitions to one day become a judge of Dachshunds, you will have to be patient, to serve your apprenticeship in the show-ring, and to prove that you really are a dedicated Dachshund lover. Serving on a committee will be a good start, and certainly offering to act as steward at their shows will give you the best experience. Although this experience and training will hopefully enable the novice to eventually pick out a good Dachshund, and possibly to later develop into a good judge of the breed, I maintain that a good judge is born, not made. We have all encountered those judges, very often so erudite in their chats about tibias, fibulas, sternums and tarsal bones, and yet, when placing the dogs in the ring will do the oddest things, and will often end up placing very

127

Beau Geste of Woodheath in show stance.

unpleasing, untypical winners. Some breeders, too, after many many years of breeding and showing will suddenly appear in the show-ring with an exhibit which you would not be at all pleased to own.

Yet there is the newcomer who may not have owned or bred Dachshunds for very long at all, but is blessed with that elusive quality, 'an eye for a dog'. Certainly, especially in selecting puppies to run on for future showing or a breeding programme, there is a wealth of knowledge that can only be acquired over the years, and with repeated handling and rearing of puppies. It may be that you look at a puppy, perhaps the small one in the litter (or the big one), and you discard it as only pet material. Suddenly one day you will see that pup standing in his run, and you will think 'Gosh, he looks just like little Willi at that age' – little Willi who became a Champion and a great sire!

Sadly there is another aspect of success in the show-ring, and that is ruthlessness. You cannot, unless you are a millionaire, keep endless numbers of dogs, and so often the puppies that you have so hopefully run on as future winners will change, and will not prove to be worth keeping. It is at this stage that so many of the erstwhile enthusiastic newcomers drop out. They cannot bear to part with little Fritz or Lottie, and they have no room for any more. In the past it was well known that many of the great names in the breeding world were hard and ruthless, and they culled any not up to their standard.

There is another solution and a sensible one. Find a good home for the ones you cannot keep. Very often there is a selfish belief that your dog will fret and pine without you, and never settle with anyone else. Sometimes, but I think very rarely, this is so, and then indeed it would be cruel to attempt to find a new home for them, but in nine cases out of ten it is wonderful how a Dachshund will settle down with a new owner, so long as they are given love and understanding, and the new owner devotes time and patience to the change-over. Very often indeed the dog could be happier if he has been a kennel dog, or one of a crowd, and he suddenly becomes a very special person in his new home.

9

Breeding

The aim of any breeder, having decided what type of Dachshund he considers the ideal, is to produce a dominant strain which is recognizable as being from his stock. So many of the great kennels have done this in the past, and looking at a dog you might be able to say, 'that is a So-and-So', or 'that is by So-and-So'. This state of affairs is achieved, not by chance, but by careful line-breeding, in-breeding or selection.

If you make a study of pedigrees in your chosen variety, you will find that many of the winners are by the same sire. This often happens in a breed, and a dog emerges who seems to be dominant in throwing progeny of a consistent, correct type, and it could be a good way to start your breeding career by obtaining a pup from that sire's lines.

It constantly surprises me how even breeders who have been 'in the game' for many years make the mistake of dashing off to use the very latest winner at stud. It would be much better to see who the sire of that winner is, and to use him on your carefully selected foundation bitch. It is a fact that in the past some of the greatest sires in the history of the breed have not themselves been the greatest winners, and in fact, many of these immortal names in our pedigrees are not even Champions, but they possessed the genetic make-up which enabled them to sire winners in litters born to bitches of different bloodlines.

In-breeding, which is frowned upon by many people, really means the mating of brother to sister, father to daughter, mother to son and so forth. Some hold the belief that such a close relationship will result in a loss of vigour, loss of intelligence or other deterioration. This is certainly not necessarily so, because all you are doing is to increase the common inheritance factors from each side, and these could be factors of strength, intelligence or stamina. In-breeding occurs very often in nature and in plant life, and so could be considered a natural behaviour pattern.

Hobbithill Grebe, Miniature Smooth bitch, by Hobbithill Blackbird of Yewlitt out of Champion Hobbithill Chiff Chaff.

Line-breeding on the other hand is breeding to less closely related lines, but with each parent having a common ancestor, for instance the grandparent being the same on each side. This is certainly more popular, and to a novice it looks much 'nicer' on paper. Try to be certain that the common ancestor was a sound animal of good temperament – this is very important.

Out-breeding means going to a completely unrelated strain, with no, or certainly very few, relatives in the pedigree. You could have great success with this mating, or it could just produce a mixture of mediocre offspring. The whole reason behind in-breeding or line-breeding is that the offspring will hopefully be of a uniform type. Looking at the pedigrees of dogs or bitches who have produced several champions in one litter, you will so often see that they are line-bred, or in-bred.

Never breed from unsound stock or unhealthy stock. Make sure before you do breed that there is a ready market for the puppies. Sensible people usually only undertake to have a litter when they particularly want to keep a puppy themselves. Never give a puppy away – human nature being what it is, it is best to try to get the proper market price for your puppy, and then hopefully the new owner will take more care of it.

I have always been a believer in line-breeding, but in order for it to work it must of course be line-breeding back to a sound, typical and respected winning line. I personally had a very fortunate lesson when I came back from South Africa to England, and started to found my line here. I went along to a Dachshund breed show in London, and there I fell in love with a little chocolate bitch who was being exhibited in a puppy class. I looked her up in the catalogue, and I saw that she was listed as Turlshill Gay Lady. I approached her breeder, who was the late Bill Pinches, of immortal Turlshill fame, and I asked him if he would sell her to me. 'No', he said, 'I think that pup has a future, and I intend to keep her, but if you like I can give you the address of someone who has a litter now by her sire, Champion Turlshill Lancelot. Today the story of Champion Turlshill Gay Lady is familiar to all Dachshund lovers who delve into past histories, and she certainly did fulfill all Bill's hopes, and went on to beat nearly every record in her day.

I went along to see the litter Bill had told me about, and I selected and booked a bitch puppy, a lovely black-and-tan who was destined to become a very precious and beloved character. When the time came, some eighteen months later, and I decided to mate her, I found a son of Champion Turlshill Lancelot, and I mated her to him – thus a half-brother and sister mating. A strain founded in this way will hopefully become dominant for the desirable characteristics and type for which you are aiming.

It is the genetic make-up of the dog or bitch which determines the type of the puppies, and it is useful to know that brothers and sisters from the same litter do not necessarily carry the same genetic pattern. It is only by trial and error, and by many test matings that the inherent characteristics will be revealed, and only the dedicated breeder will have both the time and the enthusiasm to discover all the permutations within their line.

Recessive genes can suddenly become dominant in a litter, usually because of a link up to a similar recessive gene in the mating. Zeus vom Schwarenberg, the famous German import, whose pedigree appears in the Appendix, and who is to be found in almost *all* Standard Smooth pedigrees (as well as in many pedigrees of the other coats and sizes), if one goes back far enough, was known to occasionally throw a long-haired pup in a litter from a perfectly smooth-bred bitch. In the more distant past it was known that the

A well matched brace of Miniature Long-haireds – Champion Woodheath Bismark and his litter sister Champion Woodheath Lunar Eclipse.

great Hundesports Waldmann in Germany also occasionally threw a long-haired pup. An obvious example of this recessive gene becoming dominant is the appearance, every so often, of a chocolate pup in litters from two black-and-tan parents, a fact which has been known to cause great alarm to the novice breeder.

These coats and colours are obvious, and are immediately noticeable, but of course the same rule would apply to a sudden undesirable characteristic appearing, let us say for instance, of light eyes, bad mouth, and so forth. This is when the conscientious breeder decides that it would be unwise to repeat that mating.

On the subject of in-breeding, which is usually taken to mean the mating of mother to son, father to daughter, full sister to full brother, it might be of interest to quote from one of the earliest Dachshund fanciers, Sir Everett Millais, son of the famous painter. He was a firm believer in the advantages of in-breeding, and he stated:

'A pedigree dog is not only an animal which has a pedigree (for a mongrel may have a pedigree) but which by his pedigree shows that he has been inbred enormously, but without any deterioration in quality, and the value of such a pedigree dog lies in the fact that, in comparison with a non-inbred dog, he has the power of impressing on his progeny his own form and external characteristics, which no dog has to such an extent if it is not bred on these lines'.

Obviously the same reasoning could apply to a bitch, and in the past many famous lines have been founded on an in-bred, dominant bitch; but naturally a bitch in her lifetime produces many less offspring than a well-known sire, and so the results of her dominance are less dramatic.

We have seen that in the early, foundation days of the Teckel, in order to stamp the desired Dachshund type, the German masters in-bred to a tremendous extent, but with no apparent deterioration in stamina or character.

Colour could enter into your choice of a sire. It is useful to know that red is dominant to black-and-tan, and that black-and-tan, when mated to black-and-tan *usually* produces only black-and-tan, although very occasionally there are instances of reds occuring from such a mating, as well of course as chocolates, both through a link up to a recessive gene. In order to produce dapples, one parent *must* be dappled, and it is unwise, I think, to mate dapple to dapple, as puppies with too much white can occur, and deafness can also be introduced from this mating. Dapples are permitted to have 'wall' eyes, and some people find this very attractive.

I myself bred dapples for a great many years, and during my South African days I imported a lovely chocolate dapple from the great Madame Rikovsky, and as it was one of the very first of that colour to appear on the show-bench in that country, she always caused quite a sensation. During those years I tried most combinations of colour matings. The red dapple, although popular with some, I think should be avoided, as the coat can end up by looking merely 'mothy'. The dapple colouring, in all combinations does appear to darken with age, and lose that first brilliant sparkle. It is worth mentioning here that the dapple was especially prized in Germany, as it was considered that the coat was a good camouflage whilst hunting in the forests. The dapple colouring really comes into its own in the long-haired varieties, and today there are some really beautiful examples of both silver dapples and chocolate dapples in the show-ring, several of them having gained their titles. The 1990 Welks Championship show saw the wonderful Best in Show win for

Champion Benjamin of Ralines – a great sire in his time.

a little Miniature silver dapple bitch and Mrs Barbara O'Neill's Champion Woodheath Silver Lady made history for dapples on that day.

For reds it is most important to keep dark eyes, noses and nails, known as dark 'points'. So often one sees dogs with light eyes, even in black-and-tans, and even alas, in well-known winners, and this is very undesirable. If you mate red to red for a great many generations, you could find that you are getting light, yellowish coats and then it is a good idea to introduce black-and-tan blood, in order to strengthen the pigmentation. Likewise with black-and-tans, the tan can become too pale, and sometimes it can almost disappear, with the dog losing those attractive tan markings, and here again the introduction of red blood might be advisable.

I hold the belief, but I realize that it is not generally accepted, that the colour of the Dachshund to a certain extent influences his character. This I imagine could be due to the fact that in the early days different breeds were introduced by the German foresters to develop the working capabilities of the Teckel. As we have seen there were introductions of the small German Bloodhound (which was red), the Dandie Dinmont Terrier and the small Schnauzers, to name just a few, and characteristics from these outcrosses could become apparent many generations later. I believe that the reds have a better 'nose' than the other colours, although as any Dachshund owner knows, the entire breed is really amazing in its scenting ability, especially when used for its own advantage.

Dapples are usually very happy and extrovert, as are the Wires. Those colours and coats seem not to be so choosy in their selection of friends; and to judge from the figures the wire-haired is the most popular of all the coats in Germany today, as he is much preferred by the forester, as a good worker, and he is indeed still working for them today in the forests.

Breeding is a great adventure, and if it only meant that when you mated two excellent animals together you would always produce litters of winners, there would be no excitement about it.

The Mating

When you have decided that you wish to breed from your bitch, you should make certain, so far as you can, that she is sound, and that she carries no obvious undesirable traits; that her skin and coat are healthy, and that she is fit enough to nurse and rear a sturdy litter.

Bitches vary as to the time of their first season. Sometimes they can 'come in' as early as at five or six months, whilst others do not have their first season until nine months, or even later. It is very unwise to breed from a bitch until she is about fifteen months old, which could coincide with her second or even third season. The ordeal of pregnancy and whelping might be too great a strain on a still growing bitch, so it is far better to wait until she is fully mature.

The first sign of an impending season is usually a swelling of the vulva, and if you also have a male dog in the house he will become excited, and very attached to the bitch, even before you yourself notice any change. At about this time even very clean bitches sometimes have accidents in the house, as they seem to urinate more frequently. The most important thing now to notice is the beginning of the discharge, which at first can be a pale, watery red colour, becoming more profuse and darker as the ovulation advances. Bitches 'tidy' themselves up a lot at this stage, so it is not difficult to miss the actual start of a season.

Having definitely decided that your bitch is in season, *now* is the time to ring up the owner of your selected stud dog, and to book her in to be serviced. There is really nothing more irritating to the owner of a dog than for someone to ring up late one evening, and to tell you that their bitch is in season, that tomorrow is her fourteenth day, and please can they bring her along. Believe me, it does happen.

The actual time at which a bitch is ready for the dog, and will accept him, does vary, but usually it is within the period of the ninth to the fifteenth day from commencement of 'showing colour'. Without indications to the contrary it is safe to make a date to take your bitch to the stud dog on the eleventh or twelfth day.

I have myself had bitches mated (with success) on the eighth day, and I have recently heard of a bitch being ready on the fourth day, which is *most* unusual. I also remember an occasion when I had kept a bitch kenneled away from my dogs; I let her out on the twenty-first day of her season, and on the walk back to the house on our farm in the Cape she mated herself to my very young silver dapple dog. She was red, so this was certainly not a mating I would have chosen for her, but I did not think that she would conceive at so late a date in her season, but of course she did – and we had five lovely puppies.

If the owner of the dog you have selected is an experienced breeder, you will not have to worry about the actual mating, as he will normally have it all lined up. If you have come a fair distance from home, let your bitch have an opportunity to relieve herself before you arrive at your destination. If she is a maiden she will probably be alarmed by the whole procedure, and she could become snappy, and difficult to mate, even if she is normally sweet tempered.

Unless the owner of the bitch is a very experienced breeder, I always insist on the bitch being muzzled before I let my dog attempt to mate her. A very simple device, which is quite painless and comfortable for the bitch, is to take a nylon stocking, or one leg from a pair of tights, make a loop, slip it over the bitch's muzzle, make another turn around the muzzle, under her chin, and finally tie in a bow at the top of her neck (see page 138). This can be tied quite tightly, and as nylon 'gives', it is quite harmless. Recently it has become possible to buy light cloth muzzles, and the owner of a popular stud dog would be well advised to acquire one. This precaution of muzzling the bitch is wise, because if the stud dog

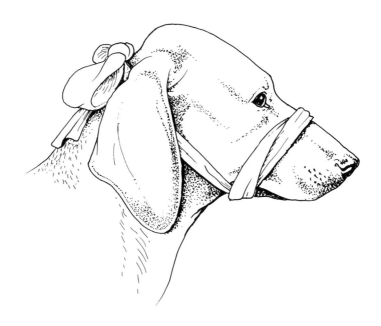

Nylon stocking used to control the bitch during mating.

gets bitten or snapped early on in his attempt to mate her, he could be completely put off, and decide not to try his luck too hard, and should he be a young and inexperienced dog, it could seriously affect his stud career.

With Miniatures it is possible to do the actual mating on a table, and I have known of Standard breeders who have done so, but usually a mating means getting down to business on the ground.

After the bitch has been muzzled (which might have to be done by the owner) if she is a very excitable one, the owner is usually asked to hold her firmly in the front, to prevent her leaping away when the dog starts to mount her, as well as reassuring her, if she is one of the nervous kind.

If the dog is experienced, he will usually just have an excited sniff at her backside, and then start to mount her. Patience is needed at this stage, for often the dog will make several attempts at mounting and trying to effect an entrance before he actually does achieve a tie. It is quite normal for the dog to behave in this manner, and I expect he likes to make the most of it, but so many owners, usually the novice ones, become impatient at this stage.

Should the dog successfully enter the bitch on several occasions, but fail to achieve a tie, it could be helpful to gently insert a disinfected finger, lubricated with a little vaseline, into the passage to try to make sure that there is no obvious obstruction. The lack of complete penetration on the part of the dog could also mean that the passage is abnormally short, thus preventing the dog from effecting the tie, but such a condition is rare.

The tie occurs when the male organ fully enters the vagina and the base of the penis becomes greatly enlarged and swollen. This swollen part, which looks like two knobs which are very hard, is held in place by the vagina, in fact firmly locked there, and it is not until the bitch releases him, that the dog can withdraw.

A mating without a tie, described as a 'slip mating', means that the dog has entered the passage and whilst *in situ* has discharged his semen but has failed to tie. This can certainly be just as successful in producing puppies as can a long lasting tie. I have had big litters several times from slip matings, and conversely no puppies from a good mating with a long lasting tie.

However, as the owner of a stud dog, I do like to see a good tie as this usually means that all was well, and that the bitch was ready. If there has just been a slip mating I decide to take no fee at this point, telling the owner of the bitch that I will take the stud fee when the bitch whelps or if a vet has confirmed her in whelp; meanwhile I will retain the green Kennel Club form, (Form 1), which must be filled in and signed by the owner of the sire of a litter before it can be registered at the Kennel Club, and I will forward this form when I receive the stud fee. This of course is a matter of personal preference. If you own a stud dog never part with the signed green form until you have the agreed fee, and if you own a bitch do make sure that you have the green form as well as a copy of the sire's pedigree when you part with the stud fee.

To return to the actual mating. When a good tie has been effected, some breeders like to 'turn' the dogs, carefully holding the animals by the tails, lifting the dog's legs up and very carefully turning him until they are standing back to back. I find that you can usually make them quite comfortable during the period of the tie by leaving them both facing forward, but by lifting the dog off the bitch's back in order to take his weight off her. However, too much interference at the early stages of the mating can cause the dog to dismount too soon, and it is advisable to try to leave them alone as much as possible, to achieve a natural mating. All dogs vary, and a stud dog

139

who is used frequently can become accustomed to being 'helped', and he will not be put off, whereas another dog may resent any help, and must be left severely alone. Once a tie has been achieved it is most important to hold and control the dogs in case they should injure themselves by struggling.

A tie can vary in time from a few minutes to twenty minutes, half an hour, or even longer, so do not be alarmed if this should occur. At this stage, with the tie achieved, the bitch, even if she has been very difficult and alarmed by the whole procedure, will quieten down, and the muzzle or stocking can usually be removed. When the mating is complete the dog and bitch will separate quite naturally, and the bitch should be picked up and carried, on her back, to rest in your car, if you have come in one. It is important that she does not relieve herself on the way.

Sometimes, if a mating is proving difficult to achieve, a useful tip I was given many years ago by an old Terrier breeder has proved helpful on many occasions. Whilst the dog is mounted on the bitch, and is endeavouring to effect an entry, take hold of the extreme tip of the bitch's vulva and very gently pull it down, this will greatly enlarge the entrance, and very often the dog will immediately glide in. At this point hold him firmly in position until a tie is achieved.

The size of the litter is determined by the bitch, not by the dog. If a dog is fertile he is capable of siring innumerable pups at any one mating. The number of pups is determined by the number of ova which are present in the bitch at the time of mating, and the maximum number should be present at the time when she shows that she is willing to mate, and is 'tailing', that is when she curls her tail away from her vulva when the dog approaches her and sniffs her backside. Some young and inexperienced bitches are slow to do this, whilst others are shameless in their display. If you own more than one dog it is much easier to discover when she is at her maximum readiness and the right day to mate her. She will play with other bitches at this time, too, so it is not necessary to own a male to find out the correct day. Failing all these helpful signs it is usually safe to stick to around the twelfth day, providing that you did not miss the onset of her season.

If you have paid your stud fee, and no puppies result from the mating, it is usual for the owner of the stud to offer you another mating to the same bitch free of charge, but these details must be agreed upon at the time of the first service.

10

Pre-Natal Care and Whelping

For five weeks or so after a successful mating, no change should be made in the diet or routine of your bitch; that is pre-supposing that she is already having a healthy, balanced diet, with plenty of fresh air and exercise.

It is usually difficult to tell whether a bitch is actually in whelp until after the fifth week from the mating date, yet, having said that, bitches vary very much in the manner in which they carry their whelps. Often a bitch, at about six weeks or so after mating, has looked enormous, and one could be forgiven for thinking that she is carrying a large litter, of eight or so pups, (which is large for a Dachshund, the average number being around five), and yet, lo and behold, when the great day arrives she produces only four pups, whereas another bitch, carrying her load high, and looking not unduly large, will go and produce a litter of nine.

Vets can usually tell whether a bitch is in whelp at about the third week after mating, after which it becomes more difficult to feel any whelps with certainty. Nowadays a great many breeders have their bitches 'scanned', but not very many vets have the equipment to do this, so it often would entail travelling a long distance, and personally I think it is an expensive luxury, unless there is a real necessity to know whether a bitch is in whelp. Bitches which have shown every sign of being in whelp, and then nearer to the time seem to get smaller, or to eventually only produce one or two pups, could have 'absorbed' the pups in the uterus. This condition, presumably due to the presence of a lethal factor, has been known, but it does not necessarily mean that a bitch who has behaved in this manner will always do so, and another time all may go well. A bitch of mine who absorbed her pups, produced a perfectly normal, healthy litter after veterinary advice.

X-rays near to the time of whelping can be helpful, especially if you are dealing with a bitch, who, from previous known history, or from some other reason (perhaps age), could run into difficulty during whelping. If she should 'pack up' after producing three pups, and X-rays have shown five *in situ*, you would know that you have to do something about it.

Your veterinary surgeon is most definitely your best friend during these weeks of pregnancy, and afterwards. As they all vary in their treatment of the in-whelp bitch, I consider it a wise move to be in touch with him or her, and to seek their advice. It is a good idea, especially if the litter is your first one, to take your bitch along to the vet about a week before she is due to whelp. At this stage it is likely that he will be able to say whether she will whelp soon, and it will alert him to the fact that a litter is imminent, and should the bitch run into difficulty, he will be more ready to come out to assist.

Worming treatment has become very sophisticated nowadays. Thankfully those hazardous times when worming a dog or puppy could literally mean its death under certain circumstances are passed. Most worm medicines today are safe and very much more effective, but do obtain them from your vet and not just from your local pet shop. Your bitch should ideally have been wormed before

Margaret Turner's Champion Marictur Black Modiste, (Sophy) eight weeks in whelp, the outcome – five pups.

you mated her, during her pregnancy, and again just after whelping. Obtain advice about these treatments, because a 'wormy' bitch will surely produce 'wormy' puppies.

Five weeks after mating you can increase the amount of food given, taking care not to make the bitch fat; the extras given should be meat, fish, or other proteins, not just extra biscuit meal. Make sure that the bitch is having sufficient calcium, now is the time to give her a daily dose. There are many good calcium powders or tablets on sale. The pups will not suffer from an inadequate diet, they will take what they need from their dam, it is the dam who will suffer, if she is not properly fed.

Once she has whelped you really cannot overfeed her. For the first two or three days after whelping she should be on a light diet of fish, chicken and lots of milk; after this you can increase her diet dramatically, with great benefit to her milk supply.

Equipment

A few weeks before the litter is due make sure that the bitch is happy and acquainted with her whelping quarters. If these happen to be away from her normal sleeping place, make her visit them and sniff around them occasionally, so that she is used to them. It is vitally important that the site you have selected and prepared for her is well away from other dogs, and that she can feel secure there.

A whelping box, bed or frame is an essential piece of equipment: properly constructed, this can save the life of newly-born puppies. These whelping places are constructed on the same lines as those used by pig breeders – there is a ledge or rail all round the inside of the box, about 2–3in (6–8cm) from the ground, which enables a pup to avoid being lain on and suffocated by the bitch. Nursing bitches are remarkably silly about this, they will lie quite happily feeding four puppies, quite oblivious to the fifth being smothered behind them, and on numerous occasions I have rescued a pup from behind, which fortunately was safely breathing under the side rail. For this reason I like, for the first week at least, to sleep somewhere within sound and reach of the litter.

Sophisticated whelping boxes can be purchased nowadays, but they are quite costly, and unless you plan to do a lot of breeding, you can construct, or get someone to construct something suitable. The whelping frame I have used for more litters than I care to

143

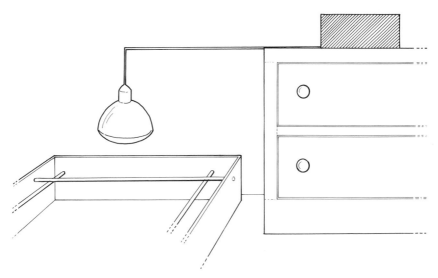

Whelping box.

remember is just a simple stout three-sided frame, about 28 × 28in (71 × 71cm), with an open front. The three sides have fitted rails for the pups to escape under, away from a careless mother. Into this frame I put veterinary-type bedding, which I cut to fit nicely inside, and under the bedding lots of newspaper to absorb the wet. Over this frame I suspend an infra-red lamp. For the actual whelping newspaper alone is the best bedding, as it can so easily just be taken away and disposed of, but we are very fortunate now in being easily able to buy this veterinary-type bedding, which is similar to that widely used in hospitals, and it can be obtained at dog shows, from advertisements in the dog papers, or from some good pet shops. It is easily washed, and it dries quickly. It can even withstand the stains and mess of the actual whelping, and will wash clean. It is perfect for the newly born pups, being warm and cosy, it absorbs all their wetting, and when they are feeding it enables them to get a grip with their little legs and prevents them slipping, doubtless avoiding hip troubles later in life. It really is a *must* for all litters.

Warmth is essential for the newly born pups, especially in winter. The ideal whelping box or bed should have an infra-red lamp suspended overhead; a safe distance so that when the bitch stands up it safely clears her back by a foot or two. This is the perfect heat for the new family, and is well worth investing in.

Champion Marictur Black Modiste after the happy event, with her family and friend.

A breeder friend of mine has an excellent arrangement in her kitchen. A cupboard under the kitchen unit lifts out when required, and into the resulting space she has fitted a whelping box, complete with safety rails. Later on, in front, when the pups start to crawl out from the nest, she erects wire panels, so that the litter then has a miniature run within the house.

The actual whelping has often been described, whether theoretically or in practice, but it cannot come amiss to discuss it again, and indeed every whelping is different, and is always exciting; that magic moment of birth, unless experienced with any creature, animal or human, is so difficult to describe. For a few delirious moments we indeed can imagine ourselves as gods, for suddenly here, warm in our hands is another creature, flesh and blood, breathing and crying, ready to live on this earth!

The period of gestation in the dog is sixty-three days, allowing one or two either side. A week early and it would be unlikely that the pups would survive, but it has been known. More than four or five days overdue and you could be in trouble, and should certainly have already sought veterinary advice. One of the early symptoms

145

that whelping is going to begin within a few days is that the vulva becomes soft and enlarged, and a discharge is usually noticed.

Miscarriages in Dachshunds are extremely rare, but they do occur. Usually they are brought about by some abnormal happening – an accident, a fall, sometimes infection, or the premature death of a whelp in the uterus. Should a miscarriage occur it is imperative to get veterinary advice, as the bitch will certainly need to have antibiotics.

Phantom pregnancies are very common in Dachshunds, whether they have been mated or not. Once the bitch has ovulated the cycle will continue – she will very often even start to produce milk, and around the time that she would have whelped she will very often go through all the symptoms of making beds and so forth even as I say, when she has *not* been mated. This can be very annoying with a show bitch, as she will lose her figure, and can also become morose and moody. Various drugs and cures are tried for this condition, but usually with little success. In the chapter on ailments I suggest the use of the drug Pulsatilla for this condition.

To return to our in-whelp bitch. If she has gone over time and you are still not certain whether or not there are any puppies there, it would be wise to have an X-ray, because there could possibly be just *one* whelp there, which has died in the uterus because it was too large for the bitch to whelp normally. Should this occur you could lose not only the whelp (which might have been saved by Caesarean section), but also the dam.

The Bitch

Bitches whelping for the first time very often make a tremendous fuss quite several hours or even days before they actually start labour proper. They cry, tear up blankets, rush around (I have even had them tear down curtains in their frenzy), scratch up their bedding and generally go berserk. This behaviour is by no means an indication of imminent whelping, or yet of dire disaster. Just try to give comfort and reassurance, and harden your heart to endure perhaps a day or more of noise and panic on the bitch's part before you need to worry. This type of behaviour does not of course always happen. I once had a little chocolate dapple who, on her first litter produced four pups with hardly a sign or a whimper in the kitchen whilst I was busy with a Monday wash. On the other hand I have had the 'curtain-puller' who raved for two days before finally being brought to bed and whelping quite easily. Every whelping is slightly different, and it is always a miracle.

One of the early indications that labour will start within twenty-four hours or so, is a drop in the bitches temperature 99°F (37°C). The normal temperature is 101.5°F (38.6°C) – higher than in humans. The temperature should be taken in the rectum. An ordinary thermometer, sterilized in a sterilizing liquid, then slightly greased, should be inserted into the rectum for about 1in (3cm), and held there for half to one minute.

At this stage, when the temperature has dropped, the bitch usually becomes quiet, she will retire to her appointed bed and settle down, sometimes panting, whining, and crying out. Usually she refuses all food, and sometimes she vomits. She looks anxiously round her at her rear, and licks the vulva, which normally has a clear discharge at this stage.

The final stage, and the most important one to notice, is when she starts to make straining, heaving motions. This is when you should make a note of the time. These heaves can continue for a few minutes, or perhaps for an hour or so before a whelp appears. The first happening after some straining 'heaves' is the appearance of the water bag, which is dark and shiny, very often mistaken for the actual whelp itself, but it is a greeny fluid, enclosed in a skin. It enlarges the passage, and facilitates the passing of a whelp. This bag will be pushed out by a final heave, will burst, and hopefully soon after a pup will emerge. Usually this first pup, as it arrives, will cause the bitch to cry out in pain, often she stands up, and allows it to finally drop out. It may still be enclosed in the membrane, or sac, and the cord from the sac will be attached to the placenta, or afterbirth, which is a greenish black, jelly-like lump.

If the bitch is behaving normally, her instinct tells her to tear open the bag which encases the whelp, allowing it to breathe; she will lick it vigorously with her tongue, and a seemingly inert whelp will then gurgle and move, and start to breathe. The bitch usually nips the umbilical cord, and sometimes she will devour the afterbirth. The eating of the afterbirth, which contains protein and minerals, is a perfectly normal function for the bitch, and whereas some breeders permit it, others make every effort to prevent the bitch doing so. I think if the bitch only eats one or two, it will do no harm, but certainly eating too many will give her diarrhoea.

Each whelp is attached to a placenta, but very often during birth the placenta becomes detached, and could be retained in the uterus, causing later complications, so it is important to try to keep an account of all afterbirths passed. This is not always possible, as so often the bitch will have eaten one without your noticing.

Should the bitch not tear open the bag and nip the cord, you must do so yourself, and do so immediately. You should have prepared yourself beforehand for all these emergencies. Your hands should have been thoroughly washed and disinfected, you should have handy sterilized scissors, cotton wool and so forth at the ready.

The bag containing the whelp is easily broken with your fingers, and as the pup emerges you must make sure that it is breathing. If it should seem lifeless massage its chest, rotate its legs and rub it all over, as the dam should have done. Normally when the whelp makes a first cry, the reluctant mother will then take over. You can nip the cord with your fingernails, or with the sterilized scissors, should the dam not do so, taking care not to cut too close to the navel, and taking care not to tug at it, as you could cause a hernia by doing so.

After the first pup has emerged, and been safely placed at a nipple to make sure that it is sucking, the next whelp could arrive quite quickly, or again it could be an hour or more before it does so. The important thing once again is to time the heaves, and should three hours ensue *after* the first heave, and no whelp arrive, it would be advisable to get veterinary advice. Complications can occur at any stage of a whelping; because one or two pups have been safely delivered, it does not follow that all the others will automatically be born safely. The bitch can become tired, and refuse to make a proper effort to heave and expel the whelp, or she can 'pack up' at any stage, and become lethargic. Veterinary help here is necessary, as injections to induce labour contractions work wonderfully.

Should a whelp appear at the mouth of the vagina, feet first, out of its bag, prompt action must be taken. Try to get the bitch to stand up (sometimes this action alone is enough to expel the whelp), take some cotton wool and grab the feet of the whelp, and try to ease it out of the passage. Place the fingers of your other hand each side of it, and *very gently* pulling downwards *as the bitch strains*. This nearly always works, and once the whelp has come, make sure that it is breathing. If it should appear lifeless, open the mouth, blow into it, massage the chest, and, should it still seem lifeless, hold it firmly in your hand and swing it vigorously up and down; this action very often starts the heart to beat. It is a good idea to hold it upside down,

148

as often fluid could have got into the lungs. Once it has heaved and made a first cry, the battle is won, and this is indeed a magic moment. Now put the whelp at a nipple, and make sure that it is sucking.

With the birth of each pup there is usually a rush of greenish bloody fluid, which is normal. Just take away the newspapers as they become stained, and put in fresh ones. Now you will be glad that you did not put the bitch on to your best blankets to whelp. Actually for a day or two *after* whelping the bitch will have a greenish discharge, normally not too much, and there is no need to be alarmed about it, unless it is profuse and continues too long.

One difficulty whilst the bitch is still whelping is that she seldom lies straight out, and therefore the pups are not easily able to get at her teats. She lies curled over in a ball, head on the newly born pups, which makes it difficult for them, unless they are very strong, to suckle easily; and some bitches, even the ones who have been wildly dependent on you and refused to let you out of their sight, once they have produced a pup and realized how wonderful motherhood is, will resent your interference, and will perhaps even growl at you, should you try to help. They always look pathetically anxious when you handle their pups at first, so now is the time to try and interfere as little as possible, provided that all appears to be going well. If each pup has had a little nourishment from the dam, and is warm and dry, there should be no cause for concern.

Sometimes it is difficult to tell when a bitch has finished whelping, as she will look very large still, but this is normal after a large litter, and it will take a day or so for her figure to come back. When you think that she has finished, give her a drink of warm milk, which has had some glucose added to it. Check that all the pups are sucking properly, as very occasionally one can be born with a cleft palate, and this condition will mean that after about three days the pup will become weak and die. It is weak, because in consequence of the cleft it has been unable to suckle properly. Often in these cases you will see the milk come out of the nostrils as it tries to suck. It is possible, by artificial feeding to keep such a whelp alive, but the possibility of operating to cure the condition in such a tiny creature is remote. Happily this is a very rare condition indeed in Dachshunds – the short-faced breeds like Bulldogs and Pekingese are more prone to this condition. This is the sort of thing that your veterinary surgeon will check when you get him along to check over your bitch after whelping. He will also make sure that none of the pups have dew claws in their hind legs, as these will have to be removed when the pup is three days old. Dew claws on the front feet, on a Dachshund, are normally left.

Aftercare

A check-up by your veterinary surgeon when you think that your bitch has finished whelping I consider well worth the expense. He will check things like cleft palates and dew claws that have been mentioned, and he will be able to tell you whether there are indeed any more pups tucked up in the uterus; he will give your bitch an antibiotic injection, and if there is any suspicion that there could be any retained afterbirths, he can give the bitch an injection to induce contractions to expel these. Better safe than sorry is a good maxim for the dog breeder.

After whelping most bitches will run a slight temperature for a few days. Remembering that a dog's *normal* temperature is 101.5°F (38.6°C), a temperature of, say, 102.5°F (39°C) is not high, one of 104°F (40°C) is high, and anything over *very* high, and help should be enlisted. Take the temperature as described before, in the rectum.

The bitch will not want to leave her puppies for a moment, if she is the normal good Dachshund mother, but she must be persuaded to go out and relieve herself – she will doubtless have to be carried out, and she will rush back to her babies as soon as possible. At this stage you can feed her liberally, it is difficult to overdo the food, especially if the litter is a large one.

Weakly, cold-feeling puppies can very often be revived by warmth. One of the best ways to achieve this is by nursing the pup next to your skin until it seems to warm up and revive, though this could take a long time.

'Fading' pups, those who just seem to lose the will to suckle, and will fade away, sometimes occur. There could be one of several causes. Sometimes acid milk is blamed, but lack of Vitamin K seems to be a possible factor. A normal, healthy, well-reared bitch should present no problems, but should puppies start to get weakly after a few days for no apparent reason, obviously veterinary help is indicated, and he may be able to save the pups by vitamin injections, and the bitch might be given injections to correct her milk content.

Orphaned whelps, or very weak ones can be tube-fed, though this is a fairly tricky procedure, as it means inserting a tube right down the oesophagus, and it needs careful instruction from your vet. Successful rearing of orphaned whelps can be achieved by bottle feeding. I have achieved this by using the special veterinary-type powdered milk, with added glucose, given via an ordinary baby feeding bottle with rubber teat, feeding every three hours, night and day to begin with. Amounts to be given are usually indicated on the tin. You find that these hand-reared pups very quickly learn to lap, so it is usually only the first two weeks that will be the hardest.

After a normal whelping, and with a good mother supplied with an adequate milk bar, the first two or three weeks are going to be your most peaceful ones, so make the most of them.

Early Days After Whelping

There is a saying in Denmark that there are as many ways to cook red cabbage as there are cooks. Indeed, as with puppies there are as many ways of feeding and rearing, as there are dog breeders.

The first priority after whelping is to the dam. You will have had her checked over by your veterinary surgeon, and now you must make sure that she is having a balanced and plentiful diet. For the first two days or so after whelping she should be on a fairly light diet, with lots of milk, which has added glucose, and chicken or fish in preference to meat for the first two days; calcium and cod liver oil should be included now and throughout the nursing period, and she should be 'wormed' once more, according to your veterinary surgeon's advice, as again, on this question, there are so many differing opinions.

The puppies must also be wormed as early as possible. The system that I have used with great success is a liquid, given in measured doses via a dropper over a period of five days, starting at about two weeks of age. I like this particular treatment, because with the 'one dose' method, (usually a pill), even if you have been very methodical, and have made quite certain that each pup has had his or her dose, there is the danger that after you have put them all back in the nest, watched them most carefully for a time, you return to find that *someone* has vomited up his dose, and you have not the faintest idea *which* one. Whereas, with the treatment I have mentioned, given over several days, all the pups will have a fair chance to get the medicine down.

Mrs Reed's Deercroft pups, aged around six weeks in their whelping quarters.

Make sure that all the teats are being used by the puppies; it is wise to feel the milk glands occasionally during those early days, to make sure that they are all soft and pliable, and not hard and congested. The dangerous one is usually the biggest teat at the end, it is normally larger than the other teats, and the new born whelps tend to neglect sucking on it, and instead go for the smaller, easier ones higher up. It is a good plan to keep putting the pups, especially the stronger ones, on to these larger teats to make sure that the milk is being drawn off. Should any of the glands become hard, and lumps be felt, bathe them with warm water, and hold hot cloths over them, and draw the milk off every now and then with your fingers. This treatment, if started early enough should cure the condition, and prevent mastitis.

A fortunately rare condition, which can occur, usually during the first two or three weeks after whelping, is parturient eclampsia, due to lack of calcium in the bitch's bloodstream. This condition can prove fatal if not immediately attended to by the veterinary surgeon, who will give subcutaneous injections. The symptoms are usually that the bitch looks dazed, might have convulsions, and she could become unconscious. Happily this *is* a rare condition, but it is best to be forewarned, as *speed is essential*. Often the victims of eclampsia are the most devoted mothers.

After about two weeks you should trim the puppies' nails; they grow very quickly, and are like little needles at first, and not only can they lacerate the milk glands and make the bitch reluctant to let them feed, but they can also scratch their siblings as they work away in the nest, and can cause sores or worse. Some pups develop little spots, especially over the head area which can be caused by the sharp nails, or can be a mild milk rash. Usually dabbing with an antiseptic is enough to banish these minor blemishes.

Eyes open at about ten days. Before this the whelps are blind and deaf, and exist only by smell and instinct. After the eyes and the ears open they will gradually start to become little personalities. The eyes usually open without any bother at all, but very occasionally an infection can get into the eye just before it opens, which could cause an abscess if neglected. The eyes will look swollen and enlarged, the pup will be in obvious discomfort, will cry constantly, and he will have no heart to suckle. Usually cotton wool, soaked in fairly hot water, which has had a little boracic acid dissolved in it, then squeezed and tested on your wrist to make sure that it is not too hot before you apply it to the eye, will ease the condition. The solution should be applied gently to the eye several times a day, and eventually this should draw out the pus. Once the pus is drawn out you will find that the swelling and the discomfort will disappear. Naturally, if you are worried, and the condition seems obstinate, seek veterinary advice. This condition, although you should be on the look out for it, is fairly rare in Dachshunds. I think it was about ten years before I personally had a case.

Make sure that the puppies' ears are kept clean. Cotton wool, dipped in warm water and antiseptic, wrung out and wrapped round a hairpin or forceps, should be used to very gently clean out the ears. Should the ears be very dirty, and appear to be causing discomfort, veterinary ear drops should be used. Ears in fact need attention all through a Dachshund's life, and should be regularly cleaned out with cotton wool and ear drops. A particular symptom of discomfort in older dogs is constant shaking of the ears.

Once the puppies' eyes have opened, and they are getting stronger on their legs, they will start to crawl out of the nest. Some develop a sense of cleanliness very early on, and prefer to relieve themselves out of the nest, so it is a good plan to put plenty of newspapers round about their early quarters, and they will then become accustomed to using the newspaper, which will be a help later on in training, and a help also for their new owner, if they are to be sold.

Weaning

Weaning the puppies should be a very gradual process, and its commencement will vary according to the size of the litter, and the milk supply of the dam. If the litter is a large one, about three weeks of age should be the time to begin, otherwise four weeks is usually soon enough. Begin with three *very* small feeds, morning, noon, and last thing at night. The first food offered should be milk. Probably the best milk to use for the first feeds, is the dried milk powder especially formulated for infant puppies, and for hand rearing, and this milk powder is obtainable from your vet or from good pet shops. The powder is re-constituted according to the directions given on the tin, and is fed at blood temperature. Glucose, and a few drops of cod liver oil should be added to the prepared feed. The first time you offer this milk feed to the pup use a medicine dropper or a teaspoon. You will soon find that the pups readily get the idea, and very soon you will be able to feed them from a saucer. Pups that are being well fed from their dam often seem reluctant to take this early feeding, but it is a good idea, nevertheless, to present the food to them, and try to get them to take a little, to get them used to the idea.

The next step in the feeding programme will be to introduce more solid food. Excellent for this purpose is one of the packaged human baby food cereals, which is mixed to a creamy consistency with milk. Normally all puppies just love this, and they will gobble it up, and will continue to like it all their lives. Now is the time, once they are guzzling into the food, to remember and observe that 'little and often' is the golden rule.

The type of milk which you use is a matter of individual choice and preference. We know that bitches milk is richer than cows milk. Goats milk will come nearest to it, and if you can easily obtain this and use it *regularly* it would be ideal. But regularly is the key word. Do not chop and change. Once you have decided on the type of milk you will use, and if it appears to suit the pups, keep to it. Many

A basketful of delightful chocolate puppies.

of my breeder friends seem to favour the use of tinned evaporated milk, mixed as per instructions, with perhaps a little glucose. I personally have always used cows milk, and have had no apparent disasters with it. I have added about a dessertspoon of glucose and $\frac{1}{2}$oz (14g) of margarine to $\frac{1}{2}$pt ($\frac{1}{3}$l) milk. Nevertheless some puppies apparently develop allergies to certain types of milk, and they get diarrhoea, so if this should occur try changing the type of milk used, and see if that clears up the condition.

During that first week of weaning, in between offering the baby cereal and milk feed, give a knob of raw meat, which has been scraped to resemble butter – a very small knob, the size of a finger-nail at first. Usually the pups love it, and they will gobble it up. For the first week of weaning therefore, alternate the milk feed with the knob of meat, making three meals a day. During the second week of weaning give five meals a day consisting of milk feed, meat, milk feed, meat, and lastly milk again. Very gradually increase the amount given; at first it will merely be a supplement to the milk which they are having from the dam.

155

After about the fourth week she will be feeding them much less, and her milk supply will gradually start to dry up. She should now be allowed to stay away from her pups as much as she likes; a normal mother will decide herself when she has had enough of them, and once she starts growling at them when they try to feed, is the time to remove her from them at night, letting her go to them only when she asks. At five weeks of age the litter should be fully weaned, except for the occasional visit from the dam, and they should be having five meals a day. The first meal given, first thing in the morning, should be a milk one; usually the baby cereal mixture. The second meal should be of minced meat, or flaked fish, minced chicken or an occasional scrambled egg mixed with a previously soaked (in stock, milk or hot water) small-sized puppy biscuit meal. There are numerous brands nowadays of these biscuit meals on the market, and as long as the one you use is from a reputable brand name, they are all good. Failing these, brown bread (wholemeal), crumbled and soaked, makes an excellent mix to the meat or fish. The third meal should be a milk one, and the fourth another meat or fish meal, with the fifth and last, given each night as late as possible. This should be another milk feed, either of the baby cereal mixture, or, as the puppy grows an excellent and well-loved meal is a crumbled up wheatflake cereal biscuit, soaked in milk. This they will love all their lives.

As soon as possible, usually from around the fourth week, get the puppies out into the air. Make them a run in a sunny part of the garden, and let them play there, just for a short time on the first occasion. Later on, when they are able to run freely, let them have as much access to the open air as possible. A simple box turned on its side, or even a large cardboard carton, with a warm blanket inside makes a useful first kennel in default of anything else.

From seven weeks onwards the pups should be ready to go to a new home. When I sell a puppy I always give the new owner a diet sheet, and about a week's supply of the foods which I have been using. A copy of that diet sheet appears in Chapter 5.

You may decide to use and to rear your pups on one of the many excellent complete foods which are now available, and in that case you need not give extra supplements, such as calcium and cod liver oil, but you will have to follow carefully the directions given by the manufacturers.

Using ordinary methods of feeding do remember to add calcium and cod liver oil to the diet. Whilst in the nest they will have been

'Perhaps this bone is a bit big for me.'

getting these vital elements via their dam, but once you start to wean them you must make sure that they are added to their food. Powdered calcium, readily available from pet shops, is an easy way of adding this vital mineral, and directions will be found on the tins. As the puppy grows the size of the meals will be increased. At about four months old you should be giving around 3oz (85g) per meat meal, thus amounting to about 6oz (170g) of meat per day, as well as the biscuit, which can soon become the adult type. As stated previously, you can chop the meat, instead of mincing it as soon as the pup is about three months old, or of course, good tinned dog meat can be used instead. At this age one of the milk feeds can be dropped, and when the puppy is about six months old give him three good meals a day. I recommend one of milk and crumbled biscuit cereal, and two of meat and biscuit meal. At twelve months old or thereabouts the dog should be having an adult diet. I give my dogs two meals a day, one in the morning usually very early, and then another in the late afternoon.

Male puppies should always be checked to ascertain whether

both testicles have descended into the scrotum. The absence of one or both testicles should be pointed out to any prospective buyer when selling a puppy. If a buyer discovers later on that the dog is a monorchid or cryptorchid, there could be some unpleasantness. The same applies to any other visible fault, such as an incorrect bite. Although these things can certainly right themselves later on, it is much better to let the prospective buyer be aware of them. You can be certain that on the first visit such a pup makes to a vet with his new owner (probably for his inoculation), he will be only too delighted to tell the novice that the pup has such a fault. How nice it is when the owner can say, 'Yes, I was told about that.'

11

Ailments and Diseases

The Dachshund when properly reared, housed and fed is normally a very healthy and sturdy dog. Fortunately for *all* canines, veterinary science has made tremendous strides, particularly since the last war, and ailments which previously had been considered incurable can now be treated, and many of the diseases, such as distemper, can be safely inoculated against.

It cannot be too highly stressed that the owner's best friend is his veterinary surgeon, and although over the years the breeder acquires much knowledge and expertise, especially in quickly recognizing danger signals, and with the recollection of past treatment is able to deal with many emergencies without calling for help, the novice must realize that *speed* is essential, should an animal become ill or be involved in an accident. Dogs go down as quickly as they can recover from illnesses, but delay in treatment is so often the fatal mistake. Good hygiene as well as good feeding is essential, as is regular washing of bedding and of the dog if necessary, although the Dachshund, especially the smooth-coated variety, seldom needs much grooming.

The Dachshund is normally an excellent feeder, so should he go off his food this is usually an indication that all is not well, especially if this lack of appetite be combined with lethargy, and perhaps a high temperature. The normal temperature of the dog (taken in the rectum) is 101.5°F (38.6°C), and just a point or two either way is no cause for alarm (although do keep an eye on it), but should the temperature rise to 103°F (39°C) veterinary help should immediately be sought.

Diarrhoea

Diarrhoea is another early warning sign of illness, but unless it persists for more than a day or so, or has blood in it, it usually passes. It can be caused by a change in diet, or by something that the dog has eaten. A good bland invalid diet can help – give just boiled rice with perhaps a little chicken or fish, and give barley water to drink. To make this boil up one tablespoon of pearl barley to one pint of water, simmer, strain and allow to cool.

Diarrhoea could also indicate that worms are present. Although your Dachshund will have been thoroughly wormed as a puppy, and thereafter at about six monthly intervals, which will usually keep him free from these parasites, they can be picked up by eating animal droppings or by eating raw rabbit or other game, and they can also occur from flea infestation.

Ticks

Dogs that are exercised in the country can pick up ticks, especially if there are sheep or cattle nearby. The actual tick is a tiny parasite, but when fastened on to the dog and sucks his blood it swells up to the size of a pea, and is a bluish colour as it is filled with blood. Never attempt to pull it out, or the head will surely be left behind, still embedded in the dog's skin, and this could fester and cause trouble. There are several ways to remove the tick – a cigarette or hot match end placed on the swollen body will usually make it release its hold, and it can then be knocked off, head and all. Methylated spirit, dabbed on, is another way of removing them. When the tick has been removed dab the place with antiseptic and keep a watch on it. Fortunately in Britain the tick rarely carries disease. In South Africa it can be a real danger, as it carries Biliary Fever, which is fatal if not treated at once. When I lived there I used to dip all the dogs once a week in a sheep dip, which I used to mix up in a bucket, and this kept them clear, not only of ticks, but of fleas and other evils. The only snag was that after a couple of times they knew the sight and sound of the dip being prepared, and when I came to use it, there was not a dog to be seen, and I had to revert to cunning to achieve my aim!

If ticks or fleas are a problem with you, nowadays there is a very excellent powder (used also for mange) obtainable from your veterinary surgeon. This powder is mixed up with water, goes a very long way, does not spoil the appearance of the coat, and will keep him free from all those types of irritant.

At certain times of year, usually in late summer, harvest mites can be a nuisance. These are minute little red mites which burrow into the dog's skin, usually on the head area, and around the eyes. They cause tiny swellings and irritation, and dabbing with antiseptic or the veterinary powder used against the ticks, will remove them.

Mange

There are two forms of mange, Sarcoptic which although contagious can be very successfully treated by bathing with anti-sarcoptic preparations, and Follicular, which is often more difficult to cure, but which is not contagious. Veterinary advice must be sought if there is any suspicion of mange. Unfortunately there are some vets who class every sort of skin trouble as mange, although very often the trouble is eczema. When mange is suspected the veterinarian will usually take a skin scraping.

Dachshunds sometimes suffer from a skin condition under the arms, a thickening and wrinkling of the skin known colloquially as 'Elephant Skin' because of its appearance. This condition is caused by the rubbing and sweating under the arms, and sometimes infection can get in, and it will spread. It can be very obstinate to cure with ordinary medicines, but there is now a lotion, obtainable from your vet and used as a shampoo, which will readily disperse it if used regularly.

Ears

Ears should be inspected regularly and carefully cleaned out with cotton wool dipped in an antiseptic, to remove any debris. Wrap the cotton wool round a cocktail stick or hairpin. Puppies especially should be inspected and their ears regularly cleaned out. Canker in the ear is caused by a tiny mite invisible to the naked eye. This condition can be extremely irritating to the dog, as well as being contagious to others. If he constantly shakes his ears and scratches at them, this could be the cause. Ear drops or canker powder, obtainable from good pet shops are often enough to cure this condition, but if it should persist obtain professional advice.

Anal Glands

Anal glands, situated low down on each side of the rectal passage, can become blocked, and this will cause irritation. Symptoms of blockage are that the dog constantly licks his backside or rubs it along the ground, and very often there is a very unpleasant smell.

The veterinary surgeon will be able to squeeze out the fluid which is blocking the glands. Some breeders are able to do this themselves, but unless you are expert in this matter damage could be caused, and professional help is advised. If neglected this condition can become septic, and is obviously very irritating to the dog.

Feet

Toe nails should be cut regularly – about once a week to keep them nice and short. Exercise and hard surfaces like roads can help wear down the nails, and indeed some dogs require little attention to their feet. You should obtain proper canine nail clippers for this job – scissors are only practical on young puppies, and here I would emphasize that nail clipping should be started from a very early age so that the dog becomes used to it. Care should also be taken not to cut too deeply, as if the quick is cut the nail will bleed, and the dog, if hurt, will be very difficult to treat on the next occasion. Should the nail bleed, dab it with a solution of permanganate of potash, and usually the bleeding will stop in a couple of minutes.

Cysts

Cysts can sometimes develop between the toes, and the first indication of this might be that the dog starts to limp, or that he constantly licks at his feet. Very often just antiseptic or benzyl benzoate dabbed on regularly will clear this condition, but extreme cases might require lancing.

Eyes

Eyes usually require little attention. Eye ointment or eye drops can be used if the eye appears bloodshot or congested. Occasionally the tear duct can become blocked, causing the eye to constantly weep, and in this case veterinary aid will be needed. Progressive Retinal Atrophy (PRA) is fortunately *not* such a problem in Dachshunds as it is in other breeds. Many of the Dachshund clubs throughout the country hold eye testing clinics at their shows, and conscientious breeders will have their stud dogs and brood bitches tested, and obtain a certificate stating that their dog is clear. When using a stud dog it would be wise to check that he has been tested, and declared free.

Teeth

Most dogs, if correctly fed, have good strong teeth. It is an advantage to give hard things for them to chew. Hard biscuits and shin bones (*never* chicken bones, lamb bones or *any* bone which might splinter) will exercise the jaws and keep the teeth in good condition. Dog toothpastes are available, and help to keep the teeth free from tartar. A powder-type paste, developed for smokers, is good if rubbed on with cotton wool, and a mixture of hydrogen peroxide and milk on cotton wool makes a good cleanser. Neglected teeth can cause abscesses, and this will perhaps first be noticed by a swelling on the face. A dog with toothache rubs his face along the ground, or against his bed. Veterinary help will be required here, perhaps for extractions and scaling of the teeth although most of these dental complications usually occur in older dogs.

Hip Dysplasia

Hip Dysplasia which can be a real problem in some breeds is happily almost non-existent in Dachshunds.

Disc Disease

To present a fair picture of specific Dachshund ills, one has to make some mention of disc disease. You could go a whole lifetime, and own many Dachshunds, and never encounter it; yet you could be the unfortunate person to have a case with your first Dachshund. I have owned, and bred Dachshunds since 1942, both in Britain and in South Africa, and I have indeed lost count of the many that have lived with me, but during that time I have only had one case of disc trouble, and the dog, after careful nursing, made a complete recovery.

Opinions do vary as to why some breeds particularly Pekingese, Corgis, Dachshunds, Cocker Spaniels, etc. are more prone to develop disc problems than other breeds. Some authorities claim an inheritance factor, whilst others blame the structure of the dog.

To try to put the latter point of view into simple terms; when a dog jumps or exercises violently the shock and jarring effect is transmitted via the body and muscles to the spine, where the intervertebral discs, with their jelly-like substance, cushion the effect and shock. The Dachshund's body is heavy and long in

163

comparison to the short length and marked angulation of his hind legs, and therefore the shock goes more rapidly to the spine than it does in the longer-legged breeds. It makes sense therefore to prevent too sudden jerking and pressure on the back – for instance never let a Dachshund run up and down stairs, and try to prevent violent jerks. Any sign of back pain or paralysis and you should immediately call for veterinary aid.

An X-ray *must* be taken to determine the degree of trouble, and in fact to make certain that it is disc trouble. There are many other forms of back trouble. Treatment can consist of complete rest (the dog should be caged), for at least three weeks, and it is important that the bowels are kept moving, and if the dog is unable to urinate, the bladder will have to be emptied. Antibiotics and cortisone are usually given to relieve pressure, and prevent infection. The dog should be on an invalid diet (boiled rice, chicken or fish and barley water). Should the dog fail to respond to nursing and medication, surgery may have to be considered.

The surgical procedure, known as 'Fenestration', and performed by a veterinary orthopaedic specialist, involves cutting a window or opening, and scooping out the defective disc material on *all* the discs which are likely to be involved. Recovery from this operation apparently takes about six weeks, and the success rate is high – usually about 91 per cent.

Some Dachshunds I have known of personally have been very successfully treated for paralysis by acupuncture; and there are some veterinary surgeons who use this method of treatment. The trouble here seems to me that it is never quite clear that the dog has recovered because of the treatment, or if he would indeed have recovered in any case.

Diabetes Mellitus

Diabetes Mellitus can sometimes occur in dogs. Symptoms are often severe loss of weight and excessive thirst. If this is suspected the dog should be taken to the vet as soon as possible for a diagnosis, and it is essential to take a sample of his urine with you. You can usually obtain a sample by putting a saucer or small bowl under the dog when she or he urinates. Diabetes can sometimes be treated by medication and diet alone as long as it is not too severe, but severe cases will require daily injections of insulin in order to control the disease.

Phantom Pregnancies

Phantom pregnancies can be a real nuisance in Dachshunds, especially if you are showing your bitch. Sometimes veterinary aid is necessary if the bitch should become generally upset and disturbed, but personally I have found that injections do little to disperse the milk bar, if that is present. The herb, pulsatilla, or an extract from this plant (the pasque flower) is used in pharmacy, and is obtainable in tablet form from most herbalists and good chemists. It has worked wonders dispelling the milk in show bitches, and is really worth trying. As I have mentioned elsewhere there are both drugs and injections which can be used to prevent a bitch from coming into season in the first place.

Coughs

Coughs want watching, if persistent; dogs can pick up kennel cough from other dogs, often at shows. Infection is spread by sneezing, but unless the dog is elderly or not very strong for some other reason, kennel cough is not usually serious, and will rapidly clear up. There is a preventative injection, but it is by no means always successful.

Stings

Some dogs seem completely unaffected by wasp or bee stings, whilst others have been known to collapse. It is wise to have antihistamine tablets handy, and the actual place of the sting or any subsequent swelling will benefit from swabbing with a solution made up of water and bicarbonate of soda (two tablespoons dissolved in a pint of water).

Fights

If the fight is not too serious banging a newspaper or yelling at the dogs might stop the fight in the early stages. Picking the aggressor up by the tail can make him release his hold, but if you are alone this can be dangerous, as the other dog may leap at you, and you might be bitten. On no account ever try to put your hand in among fighting dogs. A bucket of water flung over them, or a hose turned on, is often effective, as is a blanket thrown over them. Treat bites with antiseptic and make sure your own tetanus jabs are up to date.

General Information

I have not in this brief chapter mentioned homoeopathy; that subject would require a book by itself. Many breeders are ardent believers in it, and some veterinary surgeons practise it. Certainly herbal remedies do play an important part in animal husbandry, and we are fortunate to be able to buy many of these 'simple' remedies especially prepared for canines.

I never cease to be grateful for the great advances in veterinary science that we benefit from today. It was only in 1942 that Grayce Greenburg, the American breeder wrote: 'sooner or later all dogs contract distemper and usually before the age of six months.' At the big German hound show, held in April 1938 in Munich, it was reported that there were only forty-five Smooth Dachshunds present, not counting Miniatures, as during that year German kennels had suffered great losses owing to distemper, some of them having lost forty or fifty dogs.

My Dachshunds have given me great happiness over the years, and there are so many old friends that I remember with delight, as well as some with sadness. I will end with a little verse I wrote in the very early days of my Dachshund career, when I lost a very special little puppy from distemper:

Dear little puppy, let me not hold you,
Since science has failed, then must love let you go.
Wrapt in a shroud of my tears and prayers,
Brave little puppy, if Fate wills it so.

Dreams that I built for you – vanished to dust,
Love that I kept for you – broken by pain.
Yet maybe dear puppy, you'll wake to some dawn
Where sorrow is passed, and just joy shall remain.

Willow shall weep for you, birds sing your threnody,
Earth shall press lightly upon your dear breast,
Dream on – in the shadows where day shall not trespass,
Dream on, beloved, till I call you from rest.

12

Famous Dogs Around the World

It would be quite impossible to mention here all those great dogs who have been sent out from Britain to found kingdoms overseas. Just look at the pedigrees of most winning dogs, in all coats and sizes in say Australia, New Zealand, South Africa and so forth, and there, at the back, you will find the name of a British import.

I have always taken an interest in this aspect of the dog world, as in my breeding days in South Africa I imported four Dachshunds from Britain, two dogs and two bitches, and I remember so well the thrill and excitement of that glorious moment when you open the travelling box, and see for the first time, your precious import.

Dachshund Ambassadors

I have collected just a few pictures and a few memories of some of those ambassadors, but it is a fact that nearly all the well-known kennels in Britain will be able to tell you proudly of their famous exports.

Pictured overleaf is the famous Standard Wire dog, Champion Pondwicks Hobgoblin, was bred by Elizabeth Medley, and sent over to Dee Hutchinson in the States. He had a great show career, but his greatest claim to fame is the fact that he was to sire ninety-one Champions, out of thirty-nine different dams. Indeed a great ambassador!

Of Miniature Wires in more recent times, Zena Andrew's Champion Drakesleat Komma, who is also an American and Canadian Champion is proving a great influence, and he left several Champion offspring behind in the land of his birth.

Australia and New Zealand have been very fortunate to have had some outstanding dogs of all varieties sent out to them. One who

167

Champion Pondwicks Hobgoblin. Sire of ninety-one Champions, out of thirty-nine dams.

English, American and Canadian Champion Drakesleat Komma. Sire of thirty-six American Champions.

New Zealand and Australian Champion Marictur Black Major. A group winner, and Best in Show winner at all breed championship shows, and Dachshund of the Year winner in New Zealand.

immediately comes to mind is the black-and-tan Smooth, Australian Champion Womack Wright Royalshow, who was bred in England by Rene Gale, and sent over to Mr E. Berge Phillips in New South Wales. Not only did he have a wonderful show career, winning groups in every centre, but he went Best in Show all breeds at the Melbourne Royal – a unique achievement for a Dachshund, and he was the sire of twenty-six Champions. Mrs Bethel recently exported Hampdach Dignitary to Australia, where he has sired seven Champions. He is the son of Champion Debrita D'Arcy of Hampdach, who has sired so many winners. Also a winner in Australia, and pictured here, is New Zealand Champion and Australian Champion Marictur Black Major; he was sent out to David and Kathleen Hardwick, in New Zealand, by Margaret Turner. Di Moate's 'Dianamo' Miniature Wires have become Champions in New Zealand, Kenya, America, Zimbabwe and Jamaica.

South Africa has always been very fortunate in the quality of dogs imported from Britain. There were some early Kelvindale imports, several Silvaes, and we were fortunate in my day to have Ashdown

Bosun, who was litter brother to the great Champion Ashdown Skipper, bred by Bob Pilkington. Bosun was 'discovered' by Margaret Humphries (one of South Africa's great Dachshund personalities), living as a pet, and his owner was persuaded to let him be used at stud.

I imported South African Champion Craigmere Cassinia from Frank McSalley. He was a grandson of the famous Austrian Champion Sepperl Vom Hessenhorst, and a dominant red – he served a great many bitches of all colours, but never produced anything other than red puppies. I was lucky to import from Madame Rikovsky the little black-and-tan son of Champion Urbatz von der Howitt – South African Champion Landmark von der Howitt. I 'ordered' him before he was born, and asked her to register him as Landmark von der Howitt as Landmark is my prefix. He had a great show career, won many groups and Best in Shows, and sired many champions, and his offspring won over sixty Challenge Certificates. I also imported two bitches from Madame Rikovsky; one was a chocolate dapple, Pappillio von der Howitt,

South African Champion Landmark von der Howitt was a great winner in South Africa, and his offspring won over sixty Challenge Certificates.

170

and she was one of the first of her colouring to be seen in South Africa. Many were the startled remarks she elicited when she was benched at shows such as 'look at that little worsie – she's got skin trouble, man!' I was forced to make a big notice to put over her bench, saying, 'This is a *Dapple* Dachshund. Please do not touch!'

About this same time Ivy Hockey, in the Cape, imported a lovely black-and-tan Ashdown bitch in whelp to Nina Hill's Champion Hawkestone Matelot, and in the resulting litter there was a black-and-tan dog, Matelot of Guest, who was to be useful at stud. Ina Bush, in Port Elizabeth, purchased a puppy from me, and she became really bitten by the show bug, and went on to import several dogs; from Barbara Pugh of the Tarkottas she imported South African Champion Tarkotta Red Renoir, a litter brother to Champion Tarkotta Red Rubens, and English Champion Aravorny Early Daylight, who was bred by Trevor Peak, and who had in fact been top winning Smooth bitch for 1975 in England. Ina also imported, from Betty Beaumont of the Longanlow Dachshunds, the beautiful black-and-tan bitch, pictured here, South African Champion Longanlow Ludovica, who had a wonderful show career, going Best in Show many times.

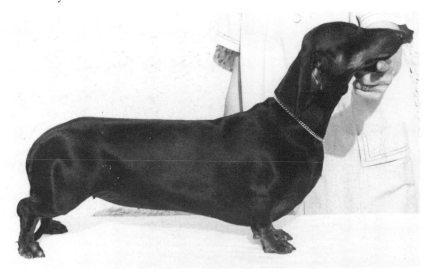

Champion Loganlow Ludovica of Allanvale. Exported to Ina Bush of the Allanvale Dachshunds in Port Elizabeth, by Betty Beaumont of the Longanlow Dachshunds. Ludovica became a great winner in South Africa, going Best in Show at many breed shows and all-breed championship shows.

171

*South African Champion, Sontag Superman of Ralines. By Champion
D'arisca Commodore out of Ralines Highland Dancer.*

*Happy basket of puppies in Trinidad. Their sire Champion (Trinidad)
Landmark Rudolph, and their dam Champion (Trinidad) Zola of
Yatesbury, both were sent out from England. Zola had a great show
career with several Best in Show wins.*

English and Indian Champion Landmark Sebastian by Deepfurrows Romeo out of Teilwood Rosie Lee.

In recent years Jean Jensen's Standard Longs have been to the fore in South Africa, as have the Africandowns, and in Miniature Longs Sunara, Wildstar, and many more. Wires have had good imports of Brockbanes, and Miniature Wires Stargangs.

In Standard Smooths Bruce Jenkins, of the Waydacks kennels in Johannesburg, was fortunate to acquire the lovely black-and-tan, who is pictured here, South African Champion Sontag Superman of Ralines. He was bred in England by Edna Cooper of the Sontag kennels, and exported by Ruth Lockett. Superman has been Best in Show all breeds, is many times a group winner, and before his departure from these shores (where he won his Junior Warrant), he sired an English Champion, and he is now siring Champions in the land of his adoption.

India, Trinidad, Barbados, Jamaica – and so many other parts of the world are all proud to welcome the Dachshund Ambassadors from our shores.

Happily the little Teckel is a most adaptable person, and he thrives in most conditions. In my experience it is never too hot for him. Just give him food, love and more food, and he is a contented chap. It might be worth mentioning here that the long-haired varieties tend to lose a great deal of their coat in the hotter climates, and the chocolates go a much lighter shade in the brilliant sunshine.

13

Conclusion

There are really six different varieties of Dachshund, and so it is difficult, unless we run into several volumes, to mention or to picture all the great names, and all the great dogs, past and present.

To get an idea of the number of Dachshunds in the show-ring today; at Crufts 1990, (when I had the privilege of judging the Smooths), there were 102 Standard Longs, 128 Miniature Longs, 71 Standard Smooths, 54 Miniature Smooths, 65 Standard Wires, and 72 Miniature Wires. That is a great number of Dachshunds, and indeed at many shows up and down the country that number is far exceeded, because at Crufts those entered are the privileged ones who, during the year have qualified to be there by having won a prize at a Championship Show.

At the recent Hound Show, held at Stafford – a great show and very popular with *all* hound enthusiasts – the Dachshund entries reflected the current popularity of the varieties. There were 75 Standard Longs, 115 Miniature Longs, 92 Standard Smooths, 93 Miniature Smooths, 63 Standard Wires and 70 Miniature Wires. This show indeed proved a great triumph for the Teckels, one of the smallest of all the hounds there, as the final accolade of Best in Show of all breeds was given to the Standard Long, Mrs Barrow's Champion Frankenwen Gold Braid, who is one of three Champions from the same litter; the reserve Best in Show was also a Dachshund – the Miniature Wire, Champion Drakesleat 'Alo 'Alo, who, coincidentally is *also* one of three Champions from the same litter. He was bred by Mrs Zena Thorn-Andrews.

We have seen from the early history of the breed how the great rise in popularity of the little Teckel occurred during the pre-war years of the 1930s, and how in those days most breeding kennels were founded directly upon imported stock, usually from the great kennels in Germany, although a few did come from other countries – Austria and Denmark were the source of a few.

During this period the Standard Smooths were the most promin

174

ent in the show-ring, as well as in the home as pets. Some great names from those early days were Madame Rikovsky (Von Der Howitt), Miss Spurrier (Querns), Mrs Huggins (Firs) Lord Wrottesley (whose dogs were always registered with two S's – Shrewd Saint, and so forth), Mrs Goodman (Roding), Miss Dixon (Kar) and many more.

In Scotland Mr Copland was an early pioneer, and he imported several very good dogs from Germany; his prefix was Orcadia, and two of his famous imports were Champion Emmo von Rautenschild, and the bitch, Champion Fifi von Alderschrofen.

The great Firs line of Mrs Huggins was largely founded upon the imported Champion Wolf vom Birkenschloss, whom Madame Rikovsky imported from Otto Pohl of Leipzig, and this little dog was to have a tremendous influence on the breed. Later Madame Rikovsky imported the immortal Champion Zeus vom Schwarenberg, as well as a string of other great dogs who were all to become famous as sires. A grandson of Zeus, her Champion Urbaz von der Howitt, was to prove a great sire in his own right. It was in this period that the Grosvenor Workmans, of Silvae fame started their great show career. They also had a team of stud dogs, and one of these, Champion Silvae Sailor's Quest, a grandson of Zeus, has gone down in history; indeed, at this time, there were over twenty of his champion offspring in the show-ring. The famous Grunwald kennels, of Mr and Mrs Lloyd were also founded upon Zeus blood, as well as Champion Kunz Schneid, and he exhibited some lovely bright red dogs.

In recent years there have been very few imports from abroad, in the Smooth world, mostly because of the great difference nowadays between the continental-type Dachshund and the British Dachshund. This is unfortunate, as I am sure that new blood would be of benefit to our lines. One of the last imports, in Standard Smooths from the Continent was in the late 1950s, when Joan Foden and Nina Hill brought over Heracles Vom Liebestraum, a small useful red dog who sired among others Champion Hawkestone Fusilier, who will be found today at the back of many pedigrees, especially the Limberins of the late Alf Hague, and the very successful Matzell kennels of the Norton family.

Today we sadly miss so many great names from our midst, although their dogs are still in our pedigrees, and are still having an influence on the breed. The Ashdown kennels of the late Bob Pilkington started just before the last war, and were at their height

Champion Rhinefields Diplomat, by Champion Silvae Virgo out of Rhinefields Catalina. Diplomat won forty-eight Challenge Certificates during his show career, and he held the record for thirteen years.

Champion Peredur Salad Days, by Champion Rhinefields Diplomat out of Peredur Souvenir.

during the 1950s, one of their greatest dogs being Champion Ashdown Skipper, who sired innumerable winners, many of whom were themselves to prove great sires. Nina Hill had many Hawkestone winners, Dorothy Spurrier was still showing Querns dogs and this period saw the first Rhinefield winners for Joyce and John Gallop, who were to produce many great dogs, one of the most famous being Champion Rhinefields Diplomat, bred on Von der Howitt lines, and a great sire himself.

More recently the Gallops bred and showed Champion Rhinefields Amala, who during her show career broke all records by winning fifty-two Challenge Certificates, under different judges. The first Womacks for Bob and Rene Gale began to appear at this time, and it was in 1962 that their famous and beautiful Champion Womack Wrightstarturn was born, and he was to prove a great sire and to have a lasting influence on the breed. Sadly Mrs Gale no longer breeds, but she still serves on many committees. In Scotland there were the Kelvindale kennels of Veronica Collins and Muriel Stewart's Dargarvels among others.

Bournemouth Champion Show, 1964, and a wonderful day for Bob and Rene Gale, pictured here with the judge, Peggy Hood Wright, as they win both the dog and bitch Challenge Certificates with the fourteen months old brother and sister champions – on the left Champion Womack Wintermorn and on the right, Champion Womack Wrightstarturn.

Champion Womack Wrum Double.

Kath and Bill Pinches were having great success at this time, and they owned Turlshill Pirate, who, although he himself was never to gain his crown, was to sire a long line of champion stock, a classic example that it is not necessarily the great winners who will prove to be the great sires. Peggy Hood-Wright's Selwoods did a lot of winning in this period, and her strain owed a lot to Champion Silvae Sailor's Quest, and to the Dachswald strain of Miss Clayton.

Ted Crowley's Aysdorn strain was founded on Turlshill Pirate, and Betty Beaumont was successfully showing her Longanlow Dachshunds, founded on Von der Howitt and Grunwald lines.

The 1970s saw the rise of several new kennels, which were to become famous, although happily during this period there were still many of the earlier breeders still with us, (Womacks, Turlshills, Rhinefields and Silvaes). Michael Triefus and his Mithril stock had a great run of success, and he bred many champions, many of whom were red, and on return from one of his overseas judging trips he brought back with him from America the black-and-tan dog, Clarion Call von Westphalen.

There were several Tarkotta champions bred by Barbara Pugh, who has had a lot of success just recently with her Miniature Longs. Lovaine Coxon of the D'Arisca prefix started to breed a string of

Champion Toffee Dapple from Tanska with Tarkotta. By Tanska Quality Street out of Torwood Chocolate Chip. Champion Toffee is the sire of the lovely silver dapple bitch, Champion Woodheath Silver Lady, bred by Barbara O'Neill, who made history for her colour and variety by going Best in Show, all breeds at WELKS 1990.

winners, carrying Womack, Silvae and Limberin bloodlines among others, her Champion D'Arisca D'Vere proving a wonderful stud. Lovaine is still with us today, and successfully campaigning her dogs. In Scotland the McNaughton's Cedavochs were prominent, and Molly Hanney had a few Dunlewey Champions.

In the mid-1970s the first Ralines were seen in the ring. Ralines is the prefix of the Lockett family; their dogs are usually shown by the daughter, Ruth, although her parents have a very active part in their breeding programme. The Ralines are founded mostly on Turlshill bloodlines, although their lovely Champion Benjamin of Ralines, who has proved a great sire, carried some other bloodlines, and his pedigree will be found in the Appendix. Today their Champion Ralines Maid to Measure has been top winning Standard Smooth for the past few years.

Mr and Mrs Rawson started to make up Rosenket champions in the 1970s, and today are very successful in the show-ring.

I made up my first English Landmark champions in this period

179

The first championship show of the Dachshund Club of Wales, held in March 1989, and the award for Best in Show goes to the black-and-tan Standard Smooth bitch, Champion Ralines Maid to Measure.

Champion Landmark Melchior. Melchior proved a great sire, and is to be found in a great many pedigrees today.

Champion Rosenket Betsie's Brigand, here seen winning Best Puppy in Show at the 1989 hound show.

Champion Debrita D'arcy of Hampdach, who has already sired five champions.

Champion Classridge Culture Club, by Champion Teilwood Fruit Polo out of Landmark Moonlight.

(after a successful show career in South Africa). The Matzells of the Norton family, the Yatesburys of Pam Sydney, the Hampdachs of Mrs Bethel, the Teilwoods of the Hensons, the Sontags of Edna Cooper, the Scawdales of Mrs Knowles, the Maricturs of Margaret Turner, the Wefans of the Websters, the Classridges of Mrs Donne-Davies – all are showing successfully today, as are the Hydax dogs of Jane Hosegood.

Happily there have been several enthusiastic newcomers to the Standard Smooth ring, and they have been achieving great things. Prominent among these are the Gatheral sisters of Phaeland fame, who are so well-known in the Long-Haired ring. They have taken up Standard Smooths with spectacular success, making up several champions in this variety in the last few years. Lyn and Malcolm Marshall of the Malynsa kennels have recently made up two champions, and we wish these newcomers great success in the future. As I have said before, with so many shows it is impossible to mention everyone here.

The Miniature Smooth

The Miniature Smooths were increasing in popularity by leaps and bounds since the introduction of separate classification and the award of their first Challenge Certificates – the first champions made up in this variety were Mrs Winder's Champion Minivale Miraculous, and Mr Negal's Champion Contessina of Montreaux – an honour that they shared in 1949. Mr Negal is still very active in the show-ring, and is producing champions all the time. Ena Bassett's Merryweather winners are at the back of many of our present day winners, as are Alf Hague's Limberins. Famous names during the 1960s were Mrs Littmoden's Wendlitts, Joan Foden's Booths, Mrs Solomon's Bowerbanks, Mrs Blandford's Flaundens, and Dr Sylvia Kershaw's great Hobbithill line was founded.

This was the period when the Kennel Club permitted the inter-breeding between coats and sizes, and studying pedigrees from this period it is interesting to come across many Standard Dachshunds in their pedigrees. This of course applied to all the other coats and sizes as well.

In the 1960s and 1970s, along with the Hobbithill's winning kennels were the Pipersvale dogs of Mrs Betty Munt. Today she is still breeding winners, and her stock goes from strength to strength.

Her Champion Pipersvale Pina-Colada is the top stud dog for his variety, and his pedigree appears in the Appendix with the pedigrees of all the top stud dogs for 1990 in each variety.

Other successful kennels were Mrs Fidler's Braishvales, Joan Foden's Booths, Mrs Nunn's Monkens, and many more. Sadly many great names from the 1970s are no longer with us, the Wimoways, the Roslayes, the Limberins, the Cannobios to mention just a few, but their names will still be found in our pedigrees. More recent names which now have become famous are the Minimeads of Gladys Mead, and the most successful Wingcrests of Mrs Batteson-Webster – her Champion Wingcrest Smart Alec has had a spectacular show career, and is proving a great sire. Mrs Blackburn's Stargangs, Mr and Mrs Newbury's Dalegarths, Mr and Mrs Voaden's Berrycourts, and Mrs Fuller's Beaudax, these are just a few, and happily the popularity of the Miniature Smooth Dachshund increases all the time, every day seeing enthusiastic newcomers enter the show-ring, and joining allegiance to this lovely variety.

The Standard Long-Hair

The Standard Long-haired Dachshund had been well established in Britain from the early days – the Long-haired Dachshund Club was formed as early as 1930, and separate classification and certificates for the breed were awarded in 1931. As with all the other varieties early stock had been imported from Germany, and the first two champions in the breed were Colonel Bedford's Champion Captain of Armadale and Champion Chloe of Armadale, both from imported stock.

Today knowing the size of all our current winning Standard Dachshunds, it might be of interest to know that the small size in imports was in no way confined to the Standard Smooths, for instance we hear that in 1934 Mrs Herdman imported the long-haired bitch, Sola von Jungfrauental (from Germany). She was black-and-tan, said to be of the highest quality, and she weighed 13lb (5.9kg). She had a litter whilst in quarantine to Blucher von Drachenburg, and the litter produced several dogs who were destined to prove valuable to the British bloodlines. One, the bitch Knowlton Madel, was to whelp the famous Champion Magdalena von Walder, for Mrs Bellamy, and who became a legendary figure in the Long-haired world. Mrs Bellamy herself imported several dogs, some of the early ones were the small Eberhart von Rälerstein, and the golden bitch, Alma von der Glonn. Mrs Smith Rewse's Primrose Patch Longs are now part of history. She bred one of the earliest champions, whose pedigree appears in the Appendix, Champion Golden Patch, and Champion Roderick of Primrose Patch, who attained his title in 1936 was by the excellent little imported dog, Champion Otter von Fels.

In the 1960s Molly Raine's Imber kennels, with such famous names as Champion Imber Coffee Bean were making their mark on the breed, Coffee Bean sired a most impressive long line of champions. Jean Jensen's Albaney stock owed a lot in those days to the Imber line (it may be of interest to note that the Imber line carried a lot of Standard Smooth blood), and her Champion Red Rebel of Albaney became one of her early successful sires. Her lovely bitch, Champion Anita Celeste of Albaney, also strongly Imber-bred, must surely be among the record holders for the dam who has produced the most winners. Today the Albaneys are still with us, and Champion Red Rheinhart of Albaney is one of the leading sires in his breed, as is Champion Red Ranger, his grandson. Between them they have sired a tremendous line of champion stock.

The 1970s saw new names added to the gallery of fame: Mrs Swann whose Swansford dogs have had a tremendous career, and broken most records, Jeff Crawfords Voryns, Mr Johnson's African-dawns, Mr and Mrs Bennett's Shardarobas, Mrs Mitchell's Bronias, Mr and Mrs Cunningham's Truanblu, Mrs Cross' Loggetas to mention a few. Sadly Dr and Mrs Raven do not breed today, (their Kennhaven dogs are still in many pedigrees), and Harry Jordan is too busy with judging engagements to continue breeding his great Danjor dogs.

Mrs Wendy Barrow's Frankanwen champions have recently been breaking all records for the breed, Champion Frankanwen Gold Braid has won several Hound Groups and has been Best in Show at All Breed shows, and she is one of three champion sisters from the same litter.

The Phaeland Longs of the Gatheral sisters are to be found in most pedigrees. Champion Phaeland Phreeranger was an outstand-ing sire, and today his grandson, Champion Mandarin of Phaeland, is taking on his mantle. Mr Fielding's Delfingi kennel is another that comes to mind. This lovely variety always looks so striking in the final line-up at a show, and on so many occasions proudly goes forward to represent and do honours for the little Dachshund.

The Miniature Long-Hair

The first Miniature Long-haired Dachshund was made up in 1949, he was Champion Marcus of Mornyvarna, bred and owned by Captain and Mrs Portman Graham. He gained his first Challenge Certificate in competition with Standard Longs. Today Miniature Longs are certainly among the most popular of the Dachshund varieties, if entries at shows are anything to go by, as they usually top the entries. Early stock was imported from the Continent, as in the other varieties, and free use was made of the then legitimate inter-breeding with other coats and sizes. Many of the breeders of Standard Longs in the early days changed their allegiance to the Miniatures, and names like Mrs Bellamy and Mrs Connell spring to mind. Those early and now famous prefixes were Mrs Stevenson's Armorel, Mrs Gwyer's Marlenwood, Mrs Connell's Von Holzner, Mrs Bellamy's Von Walder, Miss Sherer's Priorsgate, Mrs Parson's Minutist, Mrs Oswell's Mertynabbott, to name just a few.

Some of the more recent winning names are Mrs Fraser-Gibson's Sunara, Mrs Fielding's Delphik, Mr and Mrs Goddard's Minard, Mr and Mrs Corn's Rhinestar, Barbara O'Neill's Woodheath, Alan Sharman's Southcliff. Barbara Pugh's Tarkotta, Mr and Mrs Frost's Katelyn, Mrs Thomas's Shenaligh, Mrs Sanders' Sandwells, Mrs Winterbourne's Maundownes, Mr and Mrs Holland's Von Sonderwald, Mrs Skanta's Tanska, Mrs Graham's Jadag, Mr Leighton's Kizzhar, and many more. Some more recent recruits from other varieties are the Albaneys of Jean Jensen, The Kyreburns of Mrs Hoskins and the Ralines of the Lockett family, and every day new recruits join this delightful variety of Dachshund.

The Miniature Longs have recently had great success in the show-ring and in an earlier chapter I mentioned the Best in Show win of Barbara O'Neill's Champion Woodheath Silver Lady, and the wins of Champion Southcliff Starsky.

Alan Sharman's Champion Southcliff Starsky has been the leading sire in the breed for the last couple of years, and his pedigree will be found in the Appendix.

The Standard Wire

The very first Standard Wires to appear in the show-ring were all imported from Germany, and they had been in the show-ring for

186

Champion Jarthley Nabob. Nabob, a great winner in his day, was to prove a great sire, and he is to be found at the back of the pedigrees of a great many of today's winners.

Champion Woodheath Silver Lady, who made history by going Best in Show all breeds at the 1990 WELKS Championship Show.

quite a long time before they were awarded separate classification and allotted Challenge Certificates. The early pioneers of this variety in the show-ring were Mrs Howard of Seale fame, Mrs Blandy who bred and owned the great Champion Amelia, whose pedigree will be found in the Appendix, Air Vice Marshall Sir Charles lamb of the Dunkerque prefix and Miss Theo Watts. Mr Evans bred the famous Champion Wylde Enchanter, who was of largely imported stock, but his sire was the Standard Smooth, Wylde Rory, a grandson of the famous imported Champion Kunz Schneid and a son of Champion Firs Black Sheen. I only mention this because I think it is of interest to see how often in the early days permitted crossings and inter-breeding between coats and varieties took place, a custom inherited from the beginnings of our Teckel history and from the German masters, and how it was used with benefit to the breed. Today the Kennel Club has banned this practice, and any stock so bred will be ineligible for registration.

Sir Charles Lamb of the Dunkerque kennels was an early enthusiast in obedience training, and it is worth remarking here that the Wire-haired Dachshund, of all the varieties, seems to excel at this, and to get pleasure from so doing.

Mrs Quick of the great Gisbourne prefix was the breeder, among many others, of Champion Gisbourne Inca, who was owned and so successfully campaigned by Mrs Betty Farrand: Inca was to prove a great sire . . .

In Ireland Mrs Huet was the owner of the Greygates Wires, and Group Captain and Mrs Satchell bred the Orkneyingas. Miss Hoxey's Tumlows and Eric Gross' Brockbanes were also famous.

Today we have many keen breeders showing this lovely variety of Dachshund, the Grosvenor Workmans of Silvae fame, Mrs Skinner of the Ritterburgs, Mrs Naylor's Pickhills, Mrs Owen's Watermans, Miss Trim's Verwills, Mr and Mrs Brown's Teronys, Mr Derry's Andlouis, Mr Dible's Lieblings, Mr and Mrs Owen's Quitrutec, Mr and Mrs Brierley-Jones's Tulnaree, Mrs Harris's Ritlo, Miss Patton's Lesandnic, and Elizabeth Harrop's Amerfair, who incidentally used to be very successful with her Smooths.

The Miniature Wire

Miniature Wire-haired Dachshunds were the last of our six varieties to be given separate classification and to be awarded Challenge

Champion Landmark Witch Doctor, by Champion Landmark
Magician out of Landmark Brunnhilda; he was top sire in the breed
for 1988, 1989 and 1990.

Certificates, but to judge by the large number of entries and the very high standard of this little Teckel, they have really made full use of the time.

The first champion, and also the first Challenge Certificate winner was Champion Coobeg Ballyteckel Walt Weevil, a big name for a small dog, but he was to leave his mark in history. He was owned by Mrs Muriel Rhodes, of the Coobeg Dachshunds, who happily is still active today in the Dachshund world. He was bred by Mrs Besson.

Early pioneers of this variety include Mrs Alice Malony's Huntersbroad, and Sir Charles Lamb was also converted to this variety. Mrs Malony imported several dogs from Germany who were instrumental in helping to found this variety. Mrs Suzanne de Bernes of the Rigol prefix, Mrs Taylor's Bluefelt, Group Captain and Mrs Satchell's Orkneyinga, Mrs Wakefield's Sillwood, Mrs Quick's Gisbourne, Mrs Ruth Spong's Peredur, and Mrs Howard's Seale, were all early devotees.

The 1970s were to see the emergence of many famous kennels, many who happily are still with us today, and still breeding and influencing the type. Some names that should be mentioned are Miss Raphael and her Andyc dogs, Miss Elkington's Sutina kennels,

Mrs Moate's Dianamo, and Mrs Zena Thorn-Andrews whose Drakesleat kennels seem to go from strength to strength – not only have they had tremendous success in the show-ring, but her stud dogs are proving to be great sires, and the current top sire in the breed is her Champion Drakesleat Ai Say.

Several devotees from the other coats and sizes have been won over to the little Wire. A few worth mentioning are Mrs Blackburn's Stargang, Mr and Mrs Newbury's Dalegarth, Mrs Quick's Gisbourne and Mrs Grosvenor Workman's Silvae and I am sure that there will be many more.

The Dachshund Club, whose address will be found in the Appendix, publish an excellent handbook every few years wherein all the new Champions made up in the period are pictured, along with their pedigrees, and so the enthusiast is able to keep abreast of all current winners, and their breeding.

Also in the Appendix are the pedigrees of the six top winning sires for 1990 who gained that title by the fact that they had sired more winning offspring than any other dog during that period, and they were:

Dachshund, Long-haired: Champion Mandarin of Phaeland (Misses C. and S. Gatheral).
Dachshund, Miniature Long-haired: Champion Southcliff Starsky (Mr Alan Sharman).
Dachshund, Smooth: Champion Landmark Witch Doctor (Mrs Elizabeth Heesom).
Dachshund, Miniature Smooth: Champion Pipersvale Pina-Colada (Mrs Betty Munt).
Dachshund, Wire-haired: Champion Verwill Oakmaster, (Miss Veronica Trim).
Dachshund, Miniature Wire-haired: Champion Drakesleat Ai Say (Mrs Z. Thorn-Andrews).

Looking back over recent months we cannot help but be struck by the wonderful successes of our Dachshund. Nearly every coat and size of Teckel have recently won Hound Groups at All Breed Championship Shows, and the final accolade of Best in Show all breeds, has been given, on at least *six* occasions to a Dachshund.

Appendix

Important Pedigrees

PEDIGREE		

NAME   Champion Amelia

BREED   Dachshund (Wire-haired)

SEX   Bitch

COLOUR AND MARKINGS   Pepper and Salt

DATE OF BIRTH   10 April 1931

BREEDER   Mrs M. Blandy

PARENTS	GRANDPARENTS	GREAT GRANDPARENTS
SIRE Champion Achsel	**SIRE** Flott of Tavistone (born in quarantine)	**SIRE** Wicht St. George
		DAM Champion Brita of Tavistone (imported)
	DAM Anna of Nunnestall (born in quarantine)	**SIRE** Puck von Oberbuich
		DAM Daisy von Fichtenhain of Nunneshall (imported)
DAM Distel von Konigshufen (imported)	**SIRE** Sieger Hans von Konigshufen	**SIRE** Clown von Rastenberg
		DAM Fray Holle von Oetting
	DAM Dolly von Konigshufen	**SIRE** Clown von Rastenberg
		DAM Anneby von Hegeberg

PEDIGREE

NAME   Champion Golden Patch

BREED   Dachshund (Long-haired)

SEX   Bitch

COLOUR AND MARKINGS   Golden

DATE OF BIRTH   1932

BREEDER   Mrs Smith-Rewse

PARENTS	GRANDPARENTS	GREAT GRANDPARENTS
SIRE Champion Rufus of Armadale	**SIRE** German Champion Stropp von der Windberg	**SIRE** Stropp von Fuchsenstein
		DAM Pummelchen von der Berg Malepart
	DAM Elfie von Fels	**SIRE** Champion Lump von Fels
		DAM Ohni von Fels
DAM Bluebell of Armadale	**SIRE** Hengish of Armadale	**SIRE** Ratzmann von Habichrof
		DAM Edeldeude von der Waldfleur
	DAM Elfie von Fels	**SIRE** Champion Lump von Fels
		DAM Ohni von Fels

PEDIGREE

NAME   Champion Firs Black Velvet

BREED   Dachshund (Smooth)

SEX   Dog

COLOUR AND MARKING   Black and Tan

DATE OF BIRTH   June 1934

BREEDER   Mrs Basil Huggins

PARENTS	GRANDPARENTS	GREAT GRANDPARENTS
SIRE Champion Zwieback vom der Howitt	**SIRE** International Champion Wolf vom Birkenschloss (imported from Germany)	**SIRE** Champion Rotfink Schneid
		DAM Mirzl von Birkenschloss
	DAM Wohlgeboren Brunhilda	**SIRE** Champion Remagen Max
		DAM Isolde von Potte
DAM Champion Firs Chenille	**SIRE** International Champion Wolf vom Birkenschloss	**SIRE** Champion Rotfink Schneid
		DAM Mirzl vom Birkenschloss
	DAM Champion Firs Tinkergirl	**SIRE** Champion Firs Ochre
		DAM Firs Tinkerbel

PEDIGREE

NAME Champion Kunz Schneid

BREED Dachshund (Smooth)

SEX Dog

COLOUR AND MARKING Bright Red

DATE OF BIRTH 1934

BREEDER E. Pohlmey, Germany, imported by Mme. Rikovsky

PARENTS	GRANDPARENTS	GREAT GRANDPARENTS
SIRE World Champion Herr Sorge vom Seisigwald	**SIRE** Champion Erwin vom Luitpoldsheim	**SIRE** Champion Ingo vom Luitpoldsheim
		DAM Mirzl vom Luitpoldsheim
	DAM Kati Assmansheim	**SIRE** Rotschild Weidmanns-freund
		DAM Florelle Assmansheim
DAM World Champion Roselein Schneid	**SIRE** Champion Rotfink Schneid	**SIRE** Boris vom Falltor
		DAM Liri Schneid
	DAM Champion Fiffi vom Alderschroffen	**SIRE** Champion Cito vom Adlerschroffen
		DAM Erna vom Luitpoldsheim

PEDIGREE

NAME Champion Zeus Vom Schwarenberg

BREED Dachshund (Smooth)

SEX Dog

COLOUR AND MARKING Black and Tan

DATE OF BIRTH 1937

BREEDER Imported from Germany by Mme. Rikovsky

PARENTS	GRANDPARENTS	GREAT GRANDPARENTS
SIRE Cerno vom Luitpoldsheim	**SIRE** Champion Erwin vom Luitpoldsheim	**SIRE** Ingo vom Luitpoldsheim
		DAM Mirzl vom Luitpoldsheim
	DAM Linda vom Luitpoldsheim	**SIRE** Champion Erwin vom Luitpoldsheim
		DAM Freya vom Luitpoldsheim
DAM Rosemarie vom Schwarenberg	**SIRE** Champion Russ vom Luitpoldsheim	**SIRE** Champion Erwin vom Luitpoldsheim
		DAM Freya vom Luitpoldsheim
	DAM Erna vom Schwarenberg	**SIRE** Nill vom Schwarenberg
		DAM Alma vom Schwarenberg

PEDIGREE

NAME   Champion Wylde Enchanter

BREED   Dachshund (Wire-haired)

SEX   Bitch

COLOUR AND MARKINGS   Pepper and Salt

DATE OF BIRTH   11 June 1944

BREEDER   Mr H. O. Evans

PARENTS	GRANDPARENTS	GREAT GRANDPARENTS
SIRE Wylde Rory (Smooth-haired)	**SIRE** Champion Firs Black Sheen	**SIRE** Champion Zweibach von der Howitt
		DAM Champion Firs Chenille
	DAM Stecha von der Howitt	**SIRE** Champion Kunz Schneid
		DAM Firs Wishful Lady
DAM Trix of Dunkerque	**SIRE** Sports Mentor Second	**SIRE** Klausner's Mentor Second
		DAM Champion Sports Gruffa
	DAM Echo of Dunkerque	**SIRE** Champion Friedle of Seale
		DAM Ariadne of Dunkerque

PEDIGREE

NAME   Champion Silvae Sailor's Quest

BREED   Dachshund (Smooth)

SEX   Dog

COLOUR AND MARKINGS   Black and Tan

DATE OF BIRTH   June 1946

BREEDER   Mrs de Caucey Howard, owned by Mrs Grosvenor Workman

PARENTS	GRANDPARENTS	GREAT GRANDPARENTS
SIRE Champion Silvae Banjo	**SIRE** Champion Silvae Zebo	**SIRE** Champion Zeus vom Schwarenberg (imported from Germany)
		DAM Damascene of Dachswald
	DAM Linda of Oldwell	**SIRE** Burrowsdine Honey Pot
		DAM Seething Sue
DAM Champion Silvae Polish	**SIRE** Champion Silvae Zebo	**SIRE** Champion Zeus vom Schwarenberg
		DAM Damascene of Dachswald
	DAM Silvae Error	**SIRE** Firs Tally
		DAM Silvae Radium

PEDIGREE

NAME Champion Contessina of Montreux

BREED Dachshund (Miniature Smooth)

SEX Bitch

COLOUR Chocolate

DATE OF BIRTH 1947

BREEDER Mr Ivory, owned by Mr A. Negal

PARENTS	GRANDPARENTS	GREAT GRANDPARENTS
SIRE Albert August of Elfinbein	**SIRE** Prince Albert Arno	**SIRE** Arno vom Luitpoldsheim
		DAM Cara of Prince Albert
	DAM Theo of Prince Albert	**SIRE** Theo von Lindenbuhl of Ren Lak
		DAM Babette Kiven
DAM Kisska von der Howitt	**SIRE** Champion Zeus vom Schwarenberg	**SIRE** Cerno vom Luitpoldsheim
		DAM Rosemarie vom Schwarenberg
	DAM Chocoline vom der Howitt	**SIRE** Dimas Blackman
		DAM Uhea von der Howitt

PEDIGREE

NAME South African Champion Landmark von Der Howitt

BREED Dachshund (Smooth)

SEX Dog

COLOUR AND MARKING Black and Tan

DATE OF BIRTH 17 April 1953

BREEDER Mrs P. P. Rikovsky

PARENTS	GRANDPARENTS	GREAT GRANDPARENTS
SIRE Champion Urbatz von der Howitt	**SIRE** Champion Silvae Sailor's Quest	**SIRE** Champion Silvae Banjo
		DAM Champion Silvae Polish
	DAM Champion Grund von der Howitt	**SIRE** Champion Zeus vom Schwarenberg
		DAM Victoria Fidelis of Deckels
DAM Kachtan von der Howitt	**SIRE** Tzigan von der Howitt	**SIRE** Champion Zeus vom Schwarenberg
		DAM Brunislawa von der Howitt
	DAM Longview Gavotte	**SIRE** Tzigan von der Howitt
		DAM Blue Orchid of Linz

PEDIGREE

NAME   Champion Rebecca Celeste of Albaney

BREED   Dachshund (Long-haired)

SEX   Bitch

COLOUR AND MARKINGS   Red

DATE OF BIRTH   8 November 1960

BREEDER/OWNER   Mrs Jean Jensen

PARENTS	GRANDPARENTS	GREAT GRANDPARENTS
SIRE Champion Imber Café au Lait	**SIRE** Champion Imber Coffee Bean	**SIRE** Imber Black Coffee
		DAM Liza von Holzner
	DAM Liza von Holzner	**SIRE** Champion Highlight von Holzner
		DAM Suse von Fuchsenohl (imported)
DAM Anita Celeste of Albaney	**SIRE** Imber Lancer (Smooth-haired)	**SIRE** Imber Grenadier (Smooth-haired)
		DAM Imber Marie Louise (Smooth-haired)
	DAM Katherine of Albaney (Smooth-haired)	**SIRE** Imber Silversmith (Smooth-haired)
		DAM Jenn-i-fer of Albaney

PEDIGREE

NAME   Champion Womack Wrightstarturn

BREED   Dachshund (Smooth)

SEX   Dog

COLOUR AND MARKINGS   Black and Tan

DATE OF BIRTH   12 July 1962

BREEDER   Mrs Rene Gale

PARENTS	GRANDPARENTS	GREAT GRANDPARENTS
SIRE Champion Womack Wainwright	**SIRE** Turlshill Pirate	**SIRE** Champion Ashdown Skipper
		DAM Brookenville Blackbird
	DAM Womack Wagonette	**SIRE** Womack Weidmann
		DAM Womack Wunderbar
DAM Womack Winterstar	**SIRE** Womack Winterbottom	**SIRE** Champion Aysdorn Black Zenith
		DAM Womack Wagonette
	DAM Womack Angeril Jemima	**SIRE** Angeril Imperator
		DAM Angeril Daydream of Dodwhit

PEDIGREE

NAME   Champion Debrita D'Arcy of Hampdach

BREED   Dachshund (Smooth)

SEX   Dog

COLOUR AND MARKINGS   Black and Tan

DATE OF BIRTH   3 June 1985

BREEDER   Mrs T. Dixon, owned by, Mr and Mrs A. Bethel

PARENTS	GRANDPARENTS	GREAT GRANDPARENTS
SIRE Hampdach Democrat	**SIRE** Champion Womack Wrum Double	**SIRE** Champion Womack Wrightstarturn
		DAM Champion Womack Wrum Bacardi
	DAM Hampdach Lynnewood Loyalty (imported from Australia)	**SIRE** Tambo Trashad
		DAM Laen Lucinda of Hampdach
DAM Dachmargs Country Style	**SIRE** Hampdach Delegate	**SIRE** Champion Mariners Christmas Card
		DAM Hampdach Lynnewood Loyalty
	DAM Benmai Zola	**SIRE** Champion Dramatist of Rhinefields
		DAM Charanwar Geordie Girl

PEDIGREE

NAME   Champion Rhinefields Diplomat

BREED   Dachshund (Smooth)

SEX   Dog

COLOUR AND MARKINGS   Black and Tan

DATE OF BIRTH   22 October 1965

BREEDER   Mr and Mrs J. Gallop

PARENTS	GRANDPARENTS	GREAT GRANDPARENTS
SIRE Champion Silvae Virgo	**SIRE** Champion Silvae Fieldside Freelance	**SIRE** Silvae Outline
		DAM Fieldside Faith
	DAM Silvae Venus	**SIRE** Champion Silvae for Keeps
		DAM Champion Etanin of Streamside
DAM Rhinefields Catalina	**SIRE** Rhinefields Catamaran	**SIRE** Turlshill Pirate
		DAM Champion Rhinefields Melanie
	DAM Rhinefields Mercedes	**SIRE** Champion Rhinefields Lenz
		DAM Champion Rhinefields Melanie

PEDIGREE

NAME Champion Landmark Melchior

BREED Dachshund (Smooth)

SEX Dog

COLOUR AND MARKINGS Black and Tan

DATE OF BIRTH 17 November 1971

BREEDER Elizabeth Heesom

PARENTS	GRANDPARENTS	GREAT GRANDPARENTS
SIRE Longanlow Liberal	**SIRE** Amerfair Beau Brocade	**SIRE** Eastmead Doglan of Dachswald
		DAM Amerfair Sunsilk
	DAM Longanlow Lorna	**SIRE** Longanlow Lawman
		DAM Longanlow Lusamba
DAM Ortrud of Landmark	**SIRE** Launcelot of Adyar	**SIRE** Champion Turlshill Lancelot
		DAM Booth Blarney of Adyar
	DAM Rowena of Chilland	**SIRE** Champion Turlshill Lancelot
		DAM Baccante of Chilland

PEDIGREE

NAME   Champion Benjamin of Ralines

BREED   Dachshund (Smooth)

SEX   Dog

COLOUR AND MARKINGS   Black and Tan

DATE OF BIRTH   9 July 1974

BREEDER   Mr L. Price, owned by Mr and Mrs P. Lockett

PARENTS	GRANDPARENTS	GREAT GRANDPARENTS
SIRE William of Dunlewey	**SIRE** Champion Webelong Legacy	**SIRE** Champion Silvae Blueprint
		DAM Webelong Liberty
	DAM Loelia of Dunlewey	**SIRE** Loris of Dunlewey
		DAM Peri of Dunlewey
DAM Antoinette Parasio	**SIRE** Lockinvar of Westfailure	**SIRE** Champion Turlshill Highwayman
		DAM Bunjititi of Westfailure
	DAM Almondsgreen Bo-Peep	**SIRE** Almondsgreen Renown
		DAM Almondsgreen Tinkerbelle

PEDIGREE

NAME   Champion Drakesleat Ai Jail

BREED   Dachshund (Miniature Wire-haired)

SEX   Bitch

COLOUR AND MARKINGS   Brindle

DATE OF BIRTH   10 October 1976

BREEDER/OWNER   Mrs Zena Andrews

PARENTS	GRANDPARENTS	GREAT GRANDPARENTS
SIRE Drakesleat Dick Dastardly	**SIRE** Selwood Penstemon	**SIRE** Champion Bryn of Paxford
		DAM Selwood Primula
	DAM Drakesleat Silvae Mandymouse	**SIRE** Champion Witch Doctor of Cumtru
		DAM Silvae Itsamouse
DAM Champion Drakesleat Kalamity Kate	**SIRE** Champion Selwood Dittany	**SIRE** Peredur Oddjob
		DAM Selwood Buttercup
	DAM Champion Drakesleat Hussey	**SIRE** Selwood Penstemon
		DAM Drakesleat Silvae Mandymouse

PEDIGREE

NAME English, American and Canadian Champion Drakesleat Komma
BREED Dachshund (Miniature Wire-haired)
SEX Dog
COLOUR AND MARKINGS Grey Brindle
DATE OF BIRTH 13 November 1979
BREEDER Mrs Z. Andrews

PARENTS	GRANDPARENTS	GREAT GRANDPARENTS
SIRE Champion Drakesleat Rough Stuff	**SIRE** Champion Silvae Rubbermouse	**SIRE** English and New Zealand Champion Silvae Handymouse
		DAM Silvae Nuttymouse
	DAM Champion Drakesleat Riff Raff	**SIRE** Drakesleat Dick Dastardly
		DAM Champion Drakesleat Kalamity Kate
DAM Champion Drakesleat Klose Encounter	**SIRE** Champion Drakesleat Klunk Klick of Andyc	**SIRE** Champion Selwood Dittany
		DAM Champion Drakesleat Hussey
	DAM Champion Drakesleat Scarlet Woman	**SIRE** English and New Zealand Champion Silvae Handymouse
		DAM Champion Drakesleat Hussy

PEDIGREE

NAME   Champion Rhinefields Amala

BREED   Dachshund (Smooth)

SEX   Bitch

COLOUR AND MARKINGS   Black and Tan

DATE OF BIRTH   27 June 1980

BREEDER   Mr and Mrs J. Gallop

PARENTS	GRANDPARENTS	GREAT GRANDPARENTS
SIRE Champion Descendant of Rhinefields	**SIRE** Champion Rhinefields Dramatist	**SIRE** Champion Rhinefields Diplomat
		DAM Paxford Straits Black Beauty
	DAM Gailey Girl	**SIRE** Karensdale Apollo
		DAM Savanna of Beaconsfield
DAM Champion Rhinefields Amapola	**SIRE** Champion Rhinefields Diplomat	**SIRE** Champion Silvae Virgo
		DAM Rhinefields Catalina
	DAM Rhinefields Trilby	**SIRE** Jarthley Bombadier
		DAM Rhinefields Perdita

PEDIGREE

NAME Champion Pipersvale Pina-Colada

BREED Dachshund (Miniature Smooth-haired)

SEX Dog

COLOUR AND MARKINGS Red

DATE OF BIRTH 28 November 1980

BREEDER/OWNER Mrs Betty Munt

PARENTS	GRANDPARENTS	GREAT GRANDPARENTS
SIRE Champion Monksmile Dan-De-Lion	**SIRE** Irish Champion Manikin of Monksmile	**SIRE** Pipersvale Jim Dandy
		DAM Maundowne Myssion
	DAM Irish Champion Sweetmount Samantha	**SIRE** Dalegarth Gingernut
		DAM Irish Champion Mountvenus Alligator
DAM Champion Pipersvale Beaujolais	**SIRE** Champion Royal Brandy of Pipersvale	**SIRE** Champion Bowbank Drambuie
		DAM Vienda Betsy Trotwood
	DAM Champion Pipersvale Tia Maria	**SIRE** Champion Bowbank Drambuie
		DAM Pipersvale Penelope Ann

PEDIGREE

NAME   Champion Verwill Oakmaster

BREED   Dachshund (Wire-haired)

SEX   Dog

COLOUR AND MARKINGS   Black and Tan Brindle

DATE OF BIRTH   24 October 1981

BREEDER/OWNER   Miss V. Trim

PARENTS	GRANDPARENTS	GREAT GRANDPARENTS
SIRE Champion Silvae Spruce	**SIRE** Champion Watermans Whispering Pines	**SIRE** Champion Mordax Music Master
		DAM Amerfair Quite Contrary
	DAM Silvae Jollydee	**SIRE** Silvae Justice
		DAM Silvae Joyful
DAM Champion Terony Oakleigh	**SIRE** Champion Daxglade Dancing Major of Swansford	**SIRE** Champion Brockbane Red Rondo
		DAM Tumlow Crumpet
	DAM Silvae Minesasong	**SIRE** Champion Pickhill Golden Minstrel
		DAM Silvae Jollyme

PEDIGREE

NAME Champion Southcliff Starsky

BREED Dachshund (Miniature Long-haired)

SEX Dog

COLOUR AND MARKINGS Red

DATE OF BIRTH 5 September 1982

BREEDER/OWNER Mr A. Sharman

PARENTS	GRANDPARENTS	GREAT GRANDPARENTS
SIRE Champion Coobeg Rubus at Southcliff	**SIRE** Bowerbank Golden Boy	**SIRE** Youlla Silvester of Kaylyndis
		DAM Enchantment of Bowerbank
	DAM Sweet Briar of Coobeg	**SIRE** Champion Martin Martin von Holzner
		DAM Coobeg Tortoiseshell
DAM Champion Southcliff Sweet Music	**SIRE** Champion Southcliff Salvatore	**SIRE** Champion Martin von Holzner
		DAM Champion Southcliff Salome
	DAM Sunara Golden Melody of Southcliff	**SIRE** Champion Sunara Sorrento
		DAM Champion Sunara Gloire of Dijon

PEDIGREE

NAME   Champion Landmark Witch Doctor

BREED   Dachshund (Smooth)

SEX   Dog

COLOUR AND MARKINGS   Black and Tan

DATE OF BIRTH   13 July 1983

BREEDER/OWNER   Mrs E. Heesom

PARENTS	GRANDPARENTS	GREAT GRANDPARENTS
SIRE Champion Landmark Magician	**SIRE** Champion Landmark Melchior	**SIRE** Longanlow Liberal
		DAM Ortrud of Landmark
	DAM Silvae Truffle	**SIRE** Champion Silvae Rosin
		DAM Silvae Widdy
DAM Landmark Brunnhilda	**SIRE** Champion Benjamin of Ralines	**SIRE** William of Dunlewey
		DAM Antoinette Parasio
	DAM Teilwood Rosie Lee	**SIRE** Champion Landmark Melchior
		DAM Teilwood Sadie

PEDIGREE

NAME   Champion Mandarin of Phaeland

BREED   Dachshund (Long-haired)

SEX Dog

COLOUR AND MARKINGS   Red

DATE OF BIRTH   17 November 1985

BREEDER   Mr Robinson, owned by Misses C. and S. Gatheral

PARENTS	GRANDPARENTS	GREAT GRANDPARENTS
SIRE Champion Andyc Mightly Mike	**SIRE** Champion Phaeland Phreeranger	**SIRE** Champion Albaney's Red Rheinhart
		DAM Silksworth Gold Braid
	DAM Africandawns Night Milly	**SIRE** Africandawns Night Banner
		DAM Little Judy of Africandawns
DAM Jamanean Michaela	**SIRE** Champion Phaeland Phreeranger	**SIRE** Champion Albaney's Red Rheinhart
		DAM Sulksworth Gold Braid
	DAM Champion Jamanean Maria	**SIRE** Imber Cafe Paulista
		DAM Imber Cafe Rosa

PEDIGREE

NAME   Champion Drakesleat Ai Say

BREED   Dachshund (Miniature Wire-haired)

SEX Dog

COLOUR AND MARKINGS   Brindle

DATE OF BIRTH   8 June 1986

BREEDER/OWNER   Mrs Z. Thorn-Andrews

PARENTS	GRANDPARENTS	GREAT GRANDPARENTS
SIRE Champion Drakesleat Speak Easy	**SIRE** American Champion Drakesleat So to Speak	**SIRE** English, American and Canadian Champion Drakesleat Komma
		DAM Champion Drakesleat Scandal Monger
	DAM Champion Drakesleat Chit Chat	**SIRE** Champion Drakesleat Klunk Klick of Andyc
		DAM Champion Drakesleat Ai Jail
DAM Drakesleat Ai Jac	**SIRE** Champion Jack the Ripper of Drakesleat	**SIRE** Champion Silvae Crazymouse
		DAM Drakesleat Rip Off
	DAM Champion Drakesleat Ai Jail	**SIRE** Drakesleat Dick Dastardly
		DAM Champion Drakesleat Kalamity Kate

PEDIGREE

NAME   Champion Toffee Dapple From Tanska With Tarkotta

BREED   Dachshund (Miniature Long-haired)

SEX   Dog

COLOUR AND MARKINGS   Chocolate Dapple

DATE OF BIRTH   24 June 1986

BREEDER   Mr and Mrs A. N. Jury, owned by Mrs B. M. Pugh

PARENTS	GRANDPARENTS	GREAT GRANDPARENTS
SIRE Tanska Quality Street	**SIRE** Tanska Coffee 'n' Cream	**SIRE** Tanska Mr Wilhelm of Winglo
		DAM Tanska Gypsy Song
	DAM Tanska Dark Secret	**SIRE** Tanska Mr Wilhelm of Winglo
		DAM Honey of Tanska
DAM Torwood Chocolate Chip	**SIRE** Burntbarn Karribean at Tanska	**SIRE** Mertynabbot the Minstrel
		DAM Linlane Apple Blossom
	DAM Torwood Vaguely Rippled	**SIRE** Antrobus Chocolate Ripple
		DAM Torwood Variation

PEDIGREE

NAME Champion Ralines Maid to Measure

BREED Dachshund (Smooth)

SEX Bitch

COLOUR AND MARKINGS Black and Tan

DATE OF BIRTH 17 September 1986

BREEDER Mr and Mrs P. and Miss R. Lockett

PARENTS	GRANDPARENTS	GREAT GRANDPARENTS
SIRE Champion D'Arisca D'Vere	**SIRE** Champion Benjamin of Ralines	**SIRE** William of Dunlewey
		DAM Antoinette Parasio
	DAM D'Arisca Socialite	**SIRE** Plada of Deugh
		DAM Champion D'Arisca Status Symbol
DAM Ralines Helen of Troy	**SIRE** Champion D'Arisca Adventurer	**SIRE** D'Arisca Dictator
		DAM Turlshill Debutante
	DAM Champion Turlshill Leading Lady of Ralines	**SIRE** Champion Court Jester of Garelyn
		DAM Lady Jane of Turlshill

PEDIGREE

NAME   Champion Yatesbury Big Bang

BREED   Dachshund (Smooth)

SEX   Dog

COLOUR AND MARKINGS   Black and Tan

DATE OF BIRTH   22 October 1986

BREEDER   Mrs Pam Sydney

PARENTS	GRANDPARENTS	GREAT GRANDPARENTS
SIRE Champion Landmark Witch Doctor	**SIRE** Champion Landmark Magician	**SIRE** Champion Landmark Melchior
		DAM Silvae Truffle
	DAM Landmark Brunnhilda	**SIRE** Champion Benjamin of Ralines
		DAM Teilwood Rosie Lee
DAM Champion Yatesbury Nanette	**SIRE** Champion Landmark Magician	**SIRE** Champion Landmark Melchior
		DAM Silvae Truffle
	DAM Yatesbury Featherfoil	**SIRE** Womack Wroyal Raphael
		DAM Roseworth Chocolate Delight

PEDIGREE

NAME   Champion Frankanwen Gold Braid

BREED   Dachshund (Long-haired)

SEX   Bitch

COLOUR AND MARKINGS   Red

DATE OF BIRTH   20 November 1987

BREEDER   Mrs W. Barrow

PARENTS	GRANDPARENTS	GREAT GRANDPARENTS
SIRE Mandarin of Phaeland	**SIRE** Champion Andyc Mighty Mike	**SIRE** Champion Phaeland Phreeranger
		DAM Africandawns Night Milly
	DAM Jamanean Michaela	**SIRE** Champion Phaeland Phreeranger
		DAM Champion Jamanean Maria
DAM Champion Frankanwen Gold Bangle	**SIRE** Champion Frankanwen Mandrille	**SIRE** Champion Frankanwen Manhatton
		DAM Champion Frankanwen Mantilla
	DAM Frankanwen Gold Gem	**SIRE** Champion Frankanwen Black Tarquin
		DAM Champion Frankanwen Gold Spinner of Swansford

PEDIGREE

NAME Champion Andlouis' Black Knight

BREED Dachshund (Wire-haired)

SEX Dog

COLOUR AND MARKINGS Brindle

DATE OF BIRTH 24 January 1988

BREEDER Mr A. Derry

PARENTS	GRANDPARENTS	GREAT GRANDPARENTS
SIRE Champion Quitrutec Homeward Bound	**SIRE** Quitrutec Happy with You	**SIRE** Quitrutec Wheel of Fortune
		DAM Champion Quitrutec Friendly Persuasion
	DAM Love Me Truly at Quitrutec	**SIRE** Marksbury Marrow
		DAM Quitrutec True Love
DAM Andlouis' Golden Topaz	**SIRE** Ritterburg Red Rum	**SIRE** Champion Daxene Yukonly
		DAM Red Rosette of Ritterburg
	DAM Ritterburg Dark Secret	**SIRE** Champion Jymbar Rough Justice at Katelyn
		DAM Innishmaan Ebony Eyes of Ritterburg

Useful Addresses

The Kennel Club,
1–5 Clarges Street,
London W1Y 8AB
(Tel: 071 493 6651/071 629 5828)

The Dachshund Club,
Hon. Secretary   Mrs R.A.
Rawson,
Hilltops,
Ratten Row,
Langtoft,
Driffield,
North Humberside YO25 OTJ
(Tel: 0377 87344)

The Cambrian Dachshund Club,
Hon. Secretary   Mrs J.F.
Geeson,
'Abydachs', 10 Chatsworth
Road,
Irby,
Wirral,
Merseyside L61 8RX
(Tel: 051 648 6343)

The Dachshund Club of Wales,
Hon. Secretary   Miss P.M.
Davies,
23 Goodrich Crescent,
Newport,
Gwent NP9 5PE
(Tel: 0633 857639)

Eastern Counties Dachshund
Association,
Hon. Secretary   Mrs Marilyn
Cross,
17 Burgh Lane,
Mattishall,
Dereham,
Norfolk NR20 3QW
(Tel: 0362 850139)

The East Yorkshire Dachshund
Club,
Hon. Secretary   Mrs P.A.
Hancock,
Glencoe Hotel,
43–45 Marshall Avenue,
Bridlington YO15 2DT
(Tel: 0262 676818)

The Lancashire and Cheshire
Dachshund Association,
Hon. Secretary   Mrs K. Bethel,
'Lynnewood', 16 Warburton
Lane,
Partington,
Cheshire M31 4WJ
(Tel: 061 7757167)

The Long-Haired Dachshund
Club,
Hon. Secretaries   Mr and Mrs
Rowe,
6 Rhoose Road,
Rhoose,
South Glamorgan CF6 9EP
(Tel: 0446 710472)

The Midland Dachshund Club,
Hon. Secretary   Mrs Flo
Winchurch,
Brianolf Kennels,
Station Road,
Four Ashes,
Wolverhampton
(Tel: 0902 790276)

The Miniature Dachshund
Club,
Hon. Secretary   Mr Jack
Boulger,
Rorabuja, 13 Oxford Road,
Horspath,
Oxford OX9 1RT
(Tel: 08677 2596)

North Eastern Dachshund
Club,
Hon. Secretary   Mrs A.G.
Gladwin,
11 Kensington Gardens,
Darlington,
Co. Durham DL1 4NG
(Tel: 0325 467136)

The Northern Dachshund
Association,
Hon. Secretary   Mrs J. Naylor,
Crown Farm House,
Dishforth,
Thirsk,
North Yorks   YO7 3JU
(Tel: 0845 577876)

The Northern Long-Haired
Dachshund Breeders
Association,
Hon. Secretary   Mrs K.J.
Shaw,
Mellings Farm,
Sourhall Road,
Todmorden,
Lancashire OL14 7HZ
(Tel: 0706 813256)

The Scottish Dachshund Club,
Hon. Secretary   Mrs J.
McNaughton,
Cedavoch,
Balgownie,
Ayr Road,
Irvine,
Ayrshire,
Scotland
(Tel: 0294 311408)

Southern Dachshund
Association,
Hon. Secretaries   Mr and Mrs
L. Webster,
Home Farm House,
Hodsoll Street,
Near Wrotham,
Sevenoaks,
Kent
(Tel: Fairseat 823167)

The Ulster Dachshund Club,
Hon. Secretary   Mrs Joan
Patton,
31 Ashley Park,
Bangor,
County Down BT20 5RQ
(Tel: 0247 463829)

The West of England
Dachshund Association,
Hon. Secretary   Mrs Jane
Hosegood,
The Hyall,
Lyehole,
Wrington,
Avon BS18 7RN
(Tel: 0934 862416)

West Riding Dachshund
Association,
Hon. Secretary   Mr J.G.
Bennet,
Shardaroba, Silverhill Lane,
Teversal,
Nottinghamshire NG17 3JJ
(Tel: 0623 551838)

The Wire-Haired Dachshund
Club,
Hon. Secretary   Mr Paul Price,
Maxton,
Higham Road,
Tuddenham St Mary
Suffolk IP28 2SG
(Tel: 0628 714124)

Overseas Addresses

The American Kennel Club,
51 Madison Avenue,
New York NY 10010

The Dachshund Club of
America,
7540 Silvercrest Way,
Scotsdale AZ 85253

The Dachshund Club of New
South Wales,
Valdachs Park,
Treelands Close,
Glaston NSW 2159

The Dachshund Club of South
Australia,
15 McNicol Terrace,
Rosewater 5013,
South Australia

The Dachshund Club of
Queensland,
PO Box 13,
Sunnybank,
Queensland 4109,
Australia

South African Dachshund
Club,
87 Valerie Avenue,
Valeriedene,
Transvaal,
Republic of South Africa

Kennel Union of Southern
Africa,
68 Bree Street,
Cape Town 8001
Republic of South Africa

Teckel Club,
PO Box 5510,
Northlands 2116
Republic of South Africa

Index

abscess, eyes, 153
  tooth, 163
Adlerschroffen, 13, 21, 22, 26, 37, 157
Albaney, Ch. Rebecca Celeste of, 19, 200
Albert, Prince, 16
Amelia, Ch, 191
anal glands, 161, 162
Ancient Egypt, 7
Andlouis' Black Knight, Ch., 219
Ashdown, 30, 31, 169, 170, 175

badger hound, 43
barley water, 160
Basset de Race Allemande, 9
bathing, 100
beds, 92, 93, 94
benching at shows, 126
Birkenschloss, Ch. Wolf vom, 26, 37, 175
bloodhounds, 10, 136
bones, 95
breeding, 130
Buckhurst, Ch. Max of, 25
Buffon, 9
Buschkiel, Dr., 34, 35, 36

calcium deficiency, 152
Champion title, in Britain, United States and South Africa, 44
chest measurement, 41, 183
choke chains, 92, 104, 110, 111, 112
classes, 124, 125
cleft palate, 149
coat, 51, 62, 63, 65, 81, 83, 98, 133, 173
collars, 92, 104, 110, 111
colour, 9, 20, 21, 22, 26, 53, 56, 65, 71, 133, 134, 135, 136, 173
Coobeg Ballyteckel Walt Weevil, Ch., 34
coughs, 165
crates, 103
Cruft's, 23, 32, 34, 37, 174
cryptorchids, 86
cysts, 162

D'Arisca d'Vere, Ch., 179
Daake, August von, 10
  Wilhelm von, 13
Dachsbracke, 9
Dachshund Club, 15, 220
  of America, 42
Dachshunds in Germany, 37
  the United States, 42
Dachshund Rescue, 87
Dachskriecker, 9
Dandie Dinmont Terrier, 10, 62, 136
Dessaur, 17
Deutsche Teckelklub, 38
Deutschen Hunde-Verband, 38
dew claws, 50, 68, 86, 150
dewlap, 36, 53
Diabetes Mellitus, 164
diarrhoea, 159
disc disease, 163, 164
distemper, 91, 92, 96, 159, 166
Drakesleat, 174, 206, 207, 214
Dunkerque, Kiwi of, 34

ears, 56, 98, 153, 161
eczema, 161
'elephant skin', 161
Englemann, Dr. Fritz, 15
eyes, 56, 98, 153, 162

fading pups, 150
Falltor, von, 43
feeding, 88, 90, 91, 100, 101, 143
feeding bowls, 94
Feldmann, 19
fights, 165
Firs, 25, 31, 64, 175, 193
fleas, 160
Frankanwen, 174, 218
free mating, 140

Gale, Bob and Rene, 169, 177, 201
Gallop, Mr and Mrs, 177
German Teckelklub, 13
Gib-Hals, 15
Golden Patch, Ch., 192
Gravhund, 9
grooming, 98, 99, 100
Grosvenor Workman, Mrs, 28, 29, 175
ground clearance, 41, 54, 74, 75

Hampdach, 202
harvest mites, 160
Hayward, Major, 23, 25
Heracles vom Liebenstraum, 175
hip dysplasia, 163
Hobbithill, 183
homoeopathy, 166
Hood Wright, Peggy, 29, 178
Hound Show, 174
Howard, Millicent, 25
Huggins, Mrs Basil, 25, 64, 175, 193
Hundesports Waldmann, 133
hunting instincts, 14

inbreeding, 130
infra-red lamp, 94, 144
innoculations, 96, 97

Jackdaw, Ch., 20
Jamnik, 9
Jones, Major Harry, 16, 19, 20
judging, 127

kennels, 93, 94
Kensal Call Boy, Ch., 43
Kunz Schneid, Ch., 26, 175, 194

Lamb, Sir Charles, 25, 34
Landmark, 199, 204, 212
leads, 104, 110
Lichtenstein, 43
linebreeding, 131, 132
Lindenbuehl, Ch. Gernot vom, 37
Lovell, Rev. G.F., 16, 18, 20, 21
Luitpoldsheim, 43, 79

mange, 161
mastitis, 152
mating, 13, 136, 137, 138, 139, 140
milk, 154, 155
Millais, Everett, 18, 20, 133
Minivale Miraculous Ch., 32, 183
miscarriage, 146
monorchids, 86
Montreux, Ch. Contessina of, 32, 198
Mornyvarna, Ch. Marcus of, 34
muzzles, 137

nails, 98, 162
Negal, Mr Angel, 32, 33, 183
Neumarkt, Theo von, 23
nylon stocking muzzle, 137, 138

obedience training, 108
oestrum (heat), 84, 136
orphaned whelps, 150, 151
outbreeding, 131

parturient eclampsia, 152
Phaeland, Ch. Mandarin of, 213
phantom pregnancy, 146, 165

Pilkington, Bob, 30, 31, 170
Pinches, Bill, 10, 29, 132, 178
Pipersval, 31, 209
pregnancy, 141, 142, 143
Progressive Retinal Atrophy (PRA), 162
pulsatilla, 165

Ralines, 179, 216
registration certificate, 86
Remagen Max, Ch., 23, 26
Rhinefields, 177, 203, 208
Rikovsky, Madame, 25, 26, 28, 37, 134, 170
ringcraft training, 92, 122
Rosenket, 179

Schuller, Mr, 17, 22
Selwood, 29, 178
showing, 122
Sillwood, Ch. Jane of, 34
Silvae, 28, 29, 169, 175, 178, 197
sleeping quarters, 92
slip mating, 139
smell, sense of, 55, 104, 105
South African Kennel Gazette, 82
Southcliffe Starsky, Ch., 211
spaying, 84
Standard,
    American, 66
    British, 45
    German, 13
    Original British (1881), 65
stings, 165
straw, 94
stud dog, 137, 138, 139, 140
Swansford Arrandor, Ch., 31

tattoo, 39, 41
Teckel, 7

teeth, 48, 55, 58, 59, 65, 67, 84, 85, 92, 93, 95, 98, 163
temperature, 102, 147, 150, 159
testicles, 53, 66, 86, 158
ticks, 160
tie (mating), 139, 140
training, 91, 92, 95, 102, 106, 153
travel sickness, 103
Turlshill, 10, 29, 132, 178

Verwill Oakmaster, Ch., 210
Victoria, Queen, 16
Voryn's Cafe au Lait, Ch., 31

weaning, 154, 155, 156, 157
weight, 21, 25, 41, 53, 63, 64, 65, 66, 73, 74
whelping, 141, 142, 143, 144, 145, 146, 147, 148, 149
    boxes, 143, 144
Winders, Mrs E.A., 32
Womack Wrightstarturn, Ch., 177, 201
Woodheath Silver Lady, Ch., 31, 135
Woodwool, 94
Wooten, Mr Montague, 16, 20
working trials, 14, 29, 39, 41, 42, 43
worming, 87, 142, 151, 160
wrinkle, 36, 61
Wrottesley, Lord, 175
Wylde Enchanter, Ch., 196

Yatesbury Big Bang, Ch., 217

Zeus vom Schwarenberg, Ch., 28, 37, 79, 132, 175, 195
Zuchtwart, 39